IN TOUCH
WITH MOM....

IN SPIRIT!

A MEMOIR BY GILDA MIIROS

To order additional copies of this book, contact:
Palibrio
1663 Liberty Drive
Suite 200
Bloomington, IN 47403
Toll Free from the U.S.A 877.407.5847
Toll Free from Mexico 01.800.288.2243
Toll Free from Spain 900.866.949
From other International locations +1.812.671.9757
Fax: 01.812.355.1576
orders@palibrio.com
435388

IN TOUCH WITH MOM....
IN SPIRIT!

To begin with; there is no day or night.

Light is the spiritual ray that you carry with you; there is no timeline as you know it; only Universe and Eternity.

We do have a system of measurements and our Universal ethereal cycles; our chores and responsibilities.

Lightness and darkness are from your world; our sphere is radiant with energy.

GILDA MIRÓS

GILDA MIRÓS – author.

Puerto Rican Gilda Mirós has starred in films, theatre and television in Mexico, Puerto Rico and North America. Mirós was the paramount Latina radio personality with a daily four hour show via satellite between Miami, Los Angeles and New York; plus her radio programs were transmitted live from Latin America and Spain. She has narrated audio guides for The Metropolitan Museum of Art, NY; produced and narrated documentaries; one during the Vietnam War. On multiple occasions she narrated *"The Puerto Rican Day Parade"* for television in English and Spanish; she also wrote columns for *"Imagen"* NY and *"Selecta"* Magazine, Mia. As entrepreneur, she produced the 65 Anniversary of the Cuban Sonora Matancera with Celia Cruz and costars; at Carnegie Hall and Central Park in NYC. Mirós was awarded *"The Medal of the Virgin of the Providence"* by The Catholic Archdiocese of NYC. Several times awarded; *"ACE"* in NYC; and awarded *"Paoli"* and *"Agueybaná"* of Puerto Rico. She was spokesperson for the *"March of Dimes"* and *"The Eye Bank of NY,"* Also dubbed: *"Mother Angelica Live"* for EWTN Globally. In July, 2003 Gilda published ***"Celia Cruz and Sonora Matancera," "A Portrait of Puerto Rico"*** in 2005, ***"Hortense and Her Happy Ducklings,"*** Bilingual children's story, coauthored with her mother Monserrate, in 2006. ***"Memorias De Los Espiritus y MI Madre"*** in 2009, ***"Spirit Messages To My Mother"*** in 2010, ***"Mystical Wings" "It's All About The Spirit," "Alas Misticas" "Es Todo Cuestion Del Espiritu"*** 2012 Soft covers and e-Book.   www.gildamiros.com
www.facebook/gildamiros.com

Those familiar with my previous books on spiritist subjects are aware that after my short prayers every morning, my mom and our spirit guides telepathically transmit messages to me.

My mother Monserrate and other members of my spirit family; like ourselves, have lived innumerable earth lifetimes, but are currently in the spirit plane, as you and I will be someday; when we pass through the process called death. Monserrate was an exceptional trance medium since childhood; able to see, hear and speak with the spirits. She continued to receive messages from the invisible realm until her departure at the age of 90, in 2006.

My sons, my brother and I, happily shared memorable, lovely, loving moments with the spirits that visited us practically on a daily basis. Their wish is to awaken us earthlings to the reality of a more exquisite life beyond. To this day the narrative continues; I receive wise and inspiring messages from mom and our spirit mentors. This memoir is not a product of my imagination, the assertions are provable.

Last night I deliberated about how to give this book a better start; the manuscript was almost ready, but I needed something more in the opening remarks. I felt slightly anxious because it's my desire that the readers understand these memories perfectly well.

I asked for God's help, did my prayers and read the *"Gospel According To Spiritism."* Something I read touched me deeply, bringing tears to my eyes: *"Mediums are interpreters; responsible for transmitting the teachings of the spirits to mankind." Their mission is sacred, because it aims to open the horizons of eternal life."* Thus I felt very happy thinking about the wonderful work that my mother Monserrate had accomplished over the years and the extraordinary messages that reached us from the spirits; remaining with us, and that we shared with the world. I also thought of the spirit who was my sister in a previous lifetime; Helena, that from space, in 2000 located us in this immense Earth and managed to communicate with us; it was an immense feat. Our beloved Helena; brought other spirits who had shared lives with my mother, sons, brother and me, in multiple incarnations; It was a beautiful family reunion between incarnated and disembodied spirits, united by a great love; truly an unusual experience in this world. Even before mom's passing I had been receiving direct telepathic messages from Helena and from Albert; who had been my husband in a few lifetimes.

Monserrate and I had worked together on three books: *"Celia Cruz, La Sonora Matancera," "A Portrait Of Puerto Rico,"* and *"Hortense And Her Happy Ducklings,"* a bilingual children's tale written by her. In 2006, with my grief, I began to compile the book "*Memorias De Los Espiritus Y Mi Madre*", based on over sixty years of messages received through the medium, Monserrate; my mother. During those three years, while preparing the book; I received spirit messages telepathically almost daily; they were always loving messages; reassuring and advising us all, stories from spirits and encouragement for me to continue our work. Finishing that book I published the English version; *"Spirit Messages to My Mother,"* In 2012 launching *"Alas Misticas"* and *"Mystical Wings."*

My sister Helena's spirit has been a bastion in my spiritual awakening. Both mom and she have been determining factors in my progress during this incarnation; one in the physical world and the other in the spirit world; I don't know what would have become of me without their love and support. My mother sustained and stimulated me with my career and then took care of my two children, so that I could work; in Mexico, Puerto Rico and New York. She was my ray of sunshine and my spiritual pillar. I learned from her about faith and spiritism; together we made contact with the spirit world and Helena. There were so many marvelous moments of mutual development with mom and many other spirit mentors. Immediately after mom's crossing over, as I described in my earlier books; the daily telepathic messages resumed; now also from my mom; she calmed me with my grief, and encouraged me to write. To my surprise I was told that I also had a guide who assisted me with my works, his name is Gabriel; and with his help, my spirit family, and many other spirit allies, we wrote and published four books.

Getting back to my memories; I consider myself an inspired scribe medium; inspired, motivated and guided by spirits that work tirelessly and persistently; scattering divine seeds of peace and God's love on Planet Earth.

From: Posthumous Works by Allan Kardec. *(V-1)*

"Inspired Mediums" These *"mediums"* are those in which the signs are least apparent; in them the action of spirits is all intellectual, all morality, and it's revealed in life's small circumstances, as in great conceptions; in this concept we can say that everyone is a medium. The spirits who wish certain tasks, suggest to their subjects the necessary ideas; and so they are often *"mediums"* without knowing it. However they do have a vague intuition of a strange assistance

"Medium Scribes" are designated with this name to people who write under the influence of the spirits.

"Mechanical Medium" the spirit works on the hand, which it impulses to write.

"Intuitive Medium" The transmission of thought is achieved by the medium's perispirit serving as intermediary. The communicating spirit, in this case, does not act directly upon the hand to guide it; it acts upon the soul of the human with which it identifies itself and impresses its own will and ideas on it. In this situation, the intuitive medium writes voluntarily and is aware of what it's writing, although it is not its own thoughts.

After finishing my two manuscripts *(English/Spanish)* I sent them off to the printer and received the galleys; I reviewed them, while my loving spirit family continued communicating with me. The following are my most recent intuitions:

(My sister; Helena's spirit.)

Dearest little sister; we ask God for enlightenment and serenity to do our work; we also ask for health, temperament and disposition for you. There will be lovely encounters of souls that want to serve together, using any means to touch other souls. Together we will do much charity; we'll take God's word to many people, like the Apostles; we are the new messengers. Shared love is beautiful and also the union of generous souls.

Your mother Monserrate is very happy evaluating her recent incarnation; even with all its inconveniences, headaches and shortages, because she had, raised and inspired her children and later her grandchildren; plus many others. There are many grateful souls that remember and venerate her. It is a lovely gift from the Creator and a beautiful legacy to the world. She had the joy of serving, of living in spirit, of complying in spirit and of loving in spirit. At times we don't know where we're going, we march blindly, but we do march; we will not be trapped, that's the formula. Even with uncertainty we are moving, attempting to advance; we do not stop, and that has great merit. We are united by an unwavering love; and are joyful to feel this love so pure and solid, blessed by God; for centuries and centuries.

(My mother; Monserrate's spirit.)

Beloved daughter and beloved mother: *(I was her mother in a past life.)* We are a large family of kindred spirits, we love, seek and we help each other; together we can help to alleviate the sorrows of the terrestrial world. There is a union of thoughts and purposes. Praise God!

Tell dear Karym, my grandson and son; *(He was her son in a past life.)* so adored by me; that his puppy Petee accompanies me sometimes and that he plays in a beautiful park with Romy; they are good doggies. He was so kind to them, they remember him fondly. I am so happy with you my children and grandchildren, thank you. Gilda, believe me, you do love this world. There is so much to do and to see; it's just what you always liked. I'm leaving now with Helena because we have major tasks; we are on call, taking care of souls who need assistance; there are many ailing spirits. We are all nurses; your aunts Paquita and Pura, Mami and Granny Nenė; God bless you all. Sun, moon, stars and sky; all that awaits you.

March 27, 2012.

Helena's spirit:

(I heard chirping of the birds at my window) Joyful are the ears that hear the birds tweeting happily; they sing with gratitude to God and to life. Let us also sing to life, but by being productive, loving the life of service to others. Sister sometimes you want to fast forward life, but it's not possible; it's a daily process; learning, tripping, getting up and more learning.

It's the cycle of life, but how wonderful it is to learn, to know that we are doing and achieving, it's great! Most of the time, we don't know what causes things; isn't that true? In this case the light entered illuminating you, little sister; now you know the reason for your long stay here, caring for your father. *(My father who is 100 years old lives with me.)* God in his wisdom has planned it with kindness and generosity for both.

Enlightenment and progress for you Gilda; there's a lovely road, that's smooth and wide; it is your path, and very soon you'll go with your books in your arms; taking your small spotlight converted into a lantern by enlightened messengers accompanying you. Those who did not receive you will accept you and your works will be accommodated in their coffers. Now it's going to happen, yes now! The love that you planted will revert, you'll see it. Peace and love sister, thank God. There are many, many gathered here; eager to speak.

April 2, 2012.

Helena's spirit:

Peace and love Gilda; yes, it's me Helena; visiting you again with great joy. The new books are almost ready; a little more reviewing and that's all. Can you believe it? How wonderful! Thanks to the Creator and to the brothers who have assisted. God is our guide; always will be; leading us out of a narrow and cold road and taking us to eternity. Gilda dear, there is always something in the inkwell for you. Don't worry about tomorrow; your today is pretty and elaborate; tomorrow will be better. It is a question of days and months, whatever it is welcome it, because it comes with God permission; He knows what's best for us.

Every sunrise is beautiful for you, and your work; always eager to end or start, or continue; dearest there is always something for you; that's happiness, yes. There's no laziness, indifference or boredom in you, no, no! Precise ideals and realizations for the good of others; in spirit, before your birth you shouted out load: *"To serve, communications"* and God gave it to you. What could be better? It's nice to allocate love; it is a calm passion as your mom says. Little sister there is harmony; you know and feel it, it can also be seen.

April 12, 2012.

Gabriel's spirit:

In the name of Almighty God; it's been some time since we spoke last. Gilda, sister loved by all; do not despair. Finish the book; yes, it's lovely, lovely; we are happy and satisfied with your enormous effort and sacrifice; many hours you've spent on your task. God has a plan and it's big; it is one step further in the right direction. Follow your thoughts; the path is long and beautiful; wonderful flowers grow on both sides; they are your listeners. The bird's songs make you dream; and it's lovely to dream. Concentrate, continue and finish. We thank each of the entities from different levels which have contributed to this sacred work.

April 19, 2012.

Gabriel's spirit: *(At lake)*

In the name of Almighty God; you see Gilda, how the sun warms you without hurting you. It strengthens your bones and blood; there are many benefits with a few minutes of sunshine.

Thus God warms the soul, with a few moments of prayer; it strengthens us to cope with life. Albert says that you have been chosen by God and assisted by us to go on a new path of illumination to assist others. You'll know more sister! Our mission as a whole is beautiful. Vigor is needed; yes, because the cargo is heavy; and it will be deposited in due time and not before; you have learned that well. There is no doubt about your commitment with God and the enlightened entities; it is stamped there in your works and with your desire to do more and more, you'll do it, without hesitation. There will be many commitments and huge, as the Sun that shines, heats and lights you. Gilda, everything is happening according to plan. Luminosity, peace and serenity for you sister; nothing or nobody will make you stumble.

May 17, 2012.

Gabriel's spirit:

(I was finishing reviewing the galleys from the printer.)

In the name of Almighty God; I'm here at your side, inspiring and filling you with universal energy. *"You will find what you're looking for, my daughter."* Says your mother Monserrate nearby, with Helena and Albert; we all love you. Little sister, together we have done a lovely book and we will do more, with God's help and permission. We haven't spoken recently, but I can confirm that everything is wonderful; better than ever, I would say. God is our defender, our ray of light: serene and soothing; taking us by His tender and safe hand; thank you Father. Sister Gilda, I can say that you have to be very happy with what you have achieved.

Only a little bit more; but it is almost done. We do not give in; we're unified always. Push even harder when the door is heavy, press on with all your weight and strength, because it opens; oh yes! You see sister; little by little you advance, without realizing it, you are already reaching the goal. There is more, yes, there is a next step soon; we'll take it together.

Albert's spirit:

Peace and love, beloved Gilda; here I am, also writing. There is no more doubt; you know well that this is all true, it's real; it's a close and reliable communication. We ask for illumination to work, now and forever. The harvest will come, prepare yourself to receive much; in the material and the spiritual. Means there will be; as Helena says: yes, yes, yes. The messages will have another nuance.

June 23, 2012.

(The final books "Mystical Wings" and "Alas Místicas" came from the printing press)
Helena's spirit:

Peace and love dearest sister; we are happy with our work. Thank you for your willingness and devotion; all together we will continue working slowly, but with great love and peace. There are many assembled here, grateful to God and his messengers. Don't doubt, no; believe it sister. *(I picked up the books.)* You take the book in your hands and you are filled with joy; it's like hugging us. *"We worked together." (I cried while holding the books in my arms.)* Our joy is great; now you see it; you live it every day; surprises, gifts from God everywhere. There is still much to do, a lot; get to work.

You will have lots of information to investigate. Sister dearest, thank you for your tears of love, thank you for the commitment, executed with diligence; so you were in the past, and so you are now.

One must accomplish all the tasks; small or large, knowing that there is a commitment with God and with one's self. Illumination is required to see the reality of things as they are and not as we desire them. Peace, sister peace and patience, all will be done, yes. At least you are methodical and you try to comply. The rest leave it to God; He never fails us. Have you noticed? Don't worry so much, nothing will make you fail; there are no obstructions on the road, just light. With your beloved children; as with your brother; there are all small and large blessings. Prepare yourself, you'll soon take a trip, but with your base well placed. Your mother is nearby, as usual; we love you. God is generous and fair; when you least expect it; pretty pleasant gifts appear! Like Gabriel says: *"A divine drop of honey."*

July 14, 2012.

Arthur's spirit:

Gilda; I have a message for the world. Now is the time, let us get started! What is it all about? It's about the spirit! It's as clear as day; right before your eyes, plain to see; you just don't want to go there. You say: *"Correct my ways? Hell no! Love my neighbor? Why? Practice what is preached? Never! Let me be! If I die, I die; there is only one life, so let me enjoy it. What are you kidding me?"* You go on and on: but you're deadly wrong! You are dead! The living dead! There is not only one life, there are many lives. There are many lifetimes in your spirit files; you do have data stored in the Universe. Why not? There are files, data on earth, why not in the Universe? I have a question for you? What happens to the lifeless body when buried or cremated? It becomes ashes or topsoil; it transforms into something else, it does not disappear from the map; right? Now, what about the soul, energy or spirit that gave that body life? What happens upon body failure, or what you call death? Where does the soul or spirit go? Does it just disappear like a puff of smoke? Don't you wonder about that? Where are your love ones or friends that departed? Did they fade into nothingness? Do you think that their lives and loves were pointless?

I guess you don't believe in a Supreme Intelligence, or what man calls God. You do? Well do you ever think about how things *"Popped"* into being; that everything; Earth, nature, humans, came out of the blue? Do you really believe that? The *"Big Bang"* you say; but before that, what? You're an idiot! "*The Big Idiot"* Why don't you think, reflect, ponder; whatever you call it. Why are you so miserable? Or maybe why are you so indifferent? Are you happy? Why is there so much misery and conflict in this earthly world? Is there a reason for all that? But you say: *"It's just the way it is, that's all; no big deal." It's not my problem."* So you believe that there is no reason for it; it's just a result without a cause; is that right? So you believe that people suffer for no special reason; that they brought it on themselves? Well! In part you are finally right! Yes, yes, humans bring suffering into this world' creating chaos and misery with their thoughts and actions. They are the *"Doers,"* the sculptors, molding their lives; the co-creators of all the wretchedness. You and you, and you too; us, for we are one!

Yes, all of us; bringing grief to each other, with hate, lust, selfishness, greed, all that and much more. You say: *"It's hard to believe that"* You surely are *exaggerating"* You don't believe it?

Ok, let's try an experiment for a few days, even a week. Why don't you start thinking positive, sending loving thoughts towards everything and everyone that you come in touch with; try changing your attitude a bit; looking out for goodness in life and in others. I promise you that soon you will feel lighter, calmer; yes, happier; and you may even feel kindness surrounding you wherever you go. It's a great feeling; like having a good cool drink on a hot day; you will also see that people will react different towards you; they are seeing a new you, or a likeable you. Many negatives will become positives in your life; it's what they call: lucky days. Your aspirations and goals may well become true. Try it; what can you lose? It's all up to you. Stop being an Idiot!

July 16, 2012.

Arthur's spirit:

The excuses mortals make: *"I didn't mean to; I am so sorry, I won't do it again; forgive me Father"* and so on. Well it's not good enough; it's the old song and dance. Why don't you change your tune; dare!!!! No one is going to forgive you, if you don't mean it and correct it; or at least try to mend your ways. I do think it's about time; plus it is a detriment to your spiritual development; it is a stumbling block. You hurt others with your actions, words and attitude; even your vocal tone is annoying to others. Why? Why keep repeating the same ignorant actions? Do you solve anything?

No, no, on the contrary, you soil yourself; punishing your spirit.

July 17, 2012.

Unknown spirit:

Praise God in Heaven and all humans with good will; we love you Father, thank you. Unified we will all overcome obstacles of the terrestrial and our world. We want elevation; to continue growing in spirit. You are Supreme Illumination Father; we want your light and need it, to see our path fully, which is scary at times. Gilda, good friend go with clarity and certainty; taking firm steps, trusting God. Your inspirations will come frequently; messages with substance so that you can share them with the world that is moaning.

Gabriel's spirit:

In the name of Almighty God; it's Gabriel, here with Helena. You've almost completed this work, which started small but grew, as well as you; pretty it will be, and well received. We congratulate you for your devotion; soon you will release the books. Amazing isn't it? You still don't believe it; your hang-ups have limited you; but it is also part of your humility. We will write more soon; duty calls, answer. We will do much more, you're our little ally. All, all is well and it will be better, you will see it; there will be pleasant surprises for all; God is great and generous.

Helena's spirit:

Peace and love sister dearest; you've learned much! Ask for enlightenment, and you will have it to continue your works, that are a few, but smaller.

You are receiving the communications well; thank you Father. We know that they will continue; it's a sequence of blessings; a product of faith, love and prayer, but of course each one fulfills their duties. The books will touch many souls and also your words for groups that will listen; changes will occur soon. We are grateful, Father for your generosity. We are your allies, Gilda; we feel what you feel, it is not easy, we know it, but you'll have a new cycle; it's recycling; it will be your final stage.

August 2, 2012.

Albert's spirit:

It's wonderful to believe in God; to anticipate, because He always has pleasant surprises for us. Remain peaceful Gilda; you know in your soul, the value of these little books, what they represent. A negative comment is just a drop in a huge bucket. Throw away the dirty water, fill it with fresh, clean, crystal clear water, and continue with your compass; with your rhythm; so says Celia. God bless you all. Dear Gilda, it is me, Albert; my dear love. Everything is going well, calm down; you are very uneasy, calm yourself, it's your indecision, that's all; remember peace is all, in all. Your direct line to us is assured; communication you will have, and a lot there will be. How can I make you understand how easy that is; even if it seems difficult; but there is a long ways to go; let's walk! We love you.

August 3, 2012.

Albert's spirit:

You should not be so demanding in matters of earthly life because everything is so fleeting; that life slides along quickly; with many tribulations and suffering of the body and soul. All that passes by; what remains is the memory, the lesson and the purification; so we should not be so severe; in addition, upon incarnating we are warned; arriving aware of potential trials and tribulations. The soul has a presentiment of what you can expect; with your agreement or without it, you must comply with the tasks; you have to climb, scale, always advancing. Not all can overcome temptation or knock down walls of indifference, nor envy and hatred. Those entities feel resentment, pain; yes, spirit pain; there is pain of the spirit. *"The pains suffered by the spirits"* a chapter or book among many.

Every day we must take advantage of all goodness that appears; all those things that allow us to live comfortably; they are gifts, large and small. At any time there are surprises, unexpected results; good, beautiful and beneficial for all. God is benevolent; very generous, but we must do our part.

About the pain of the spirit; Gilda write: the spirit has an ethereal body: a fluidic and energy body which is the intermediary between the soul and the body; called perispirit; which is more or less dense, according to its evolution and circumstances. This fluid body precedes the human body, choosing any appearance it prefers; plus it consistently receives and transmits rays of energy in different shapes and capabilities. This ethereal entity collects impressions; signals or frequencies from the corporeal world that it visits regularly; again depending on its evolution and spiritual progress. It visits the planets, usually Earth; attracted by beloved incarnates that still live there. It is able to perceive and feel in its soul; in its inner spirit self, the pains and sufferings of humans; mostly of beloved incarnates. Understanding human trials and tribulations, the spirit identifies with the suffering of others, and it guides and helps; relieving and in part cleaning the negative energy that surrounds their auras. It's like cleaning the neighbor's patio. Peace and love.

August 4, 2012.

Gabriel's spirit:

In the name of Almighty God; Gilda, good woman, your name is sounding and has sounded for being tireless, persistent and a believer. Many do not believe your energy and determination; beautiful, beautiful. Let's continue until they listen; that is our purpose; to penetrate these dense brains, heavy bodies and restless minds; but we are achieving something, drop by drop. We are all happy; the promotion; it's going far, very far; Gilda, you have done wonders with what little you have; you'll do much more, but with comfort to continue working and sharing good advice from the guides; it is your mission. So it is and so it will be.

August 6, 2012.

Albert's spirit:

Enlightenment and progress Gilda and for all those present here; blessings to you; especially for the pretty and good little girl. *(My granddaughter; Vienna Skye)* You will all achieve your goals, because you are believers, noble, decent and disciplined. Clarity, joy, peace and love always, sister. No sadness, no; only love and happiness for what we have done and will do. Illumination, ask for enlightenment. Listen, Celia achieved it; God bless her. She has great spiritual strength; and has earned it; also her people's love is great and it impulses her. How wonderful it is to believe in God. Let me tell you Gilda, my beloved, Celia helped you to find her recordings in the files, for the radio show in her honor.

August 7, 2012.

Gabriel's spirit:

In the name of Almighty God; Gilda nothing is still; everything is moving, just like your cells, your tissues, the beating of your heart; all has its own rhythm and harmony; divine wisdom in each one of us; all with its tempo. God, Merciful Father, Supreme Intelligence, supplies us with everything with need; the problem lies in human beings being ungrateful, dissidents and blind. They suffer and make others suffer, with their blindness and unreciprocated love. The consequences arise very tangibly, with diseases, pains, long term suffering which is perpetuated. They ask repeatedly: for what reason? Why me? They can say: Why not me? I've abused this body; I've battered what God gave me healthy.

My myopic spirit has not been able to see anything, nothing. The cries are many and everywhere the supplication is heard at the time of pain; however no sound of praise to God at the moment of joy; or moments of material good fortune and blessings. We hear many pleas, requesting assistance; and it happens, it occurs, because God is merciful, merciful, fair and generous; the best Father. He rescues his haughty and pampered children. Assistance arrives, it always arrives.

August 8, 2012.

Albert's spirit:

We don't know why things happen, it is an enigma in most cases and we must comply with the events; but there are times when if we knew, we could accept and appreciate what is happening or what has happened for our benefit; that happened to you Gilda.

Upon reviewing your past, you will understand many things of great importance; it's like a diagram drawn by God and the enlightened entities, for your sake, for your spiritual development. It has been a painful road, but also of great importance and benefit for you and your brothers on Earth. You have given them some beautiful memories; also faith, hope and reason to believe in God and eternal life; that has great value. Rejoice, cheer up, and groom yourself happily; follow your path.

August 10, 2012.   *(Automatic writing)*

Albert's spirit:
I can write; peace and love Gilda; It's Albert.

Gilda:
Let's try to write something more, you tell me; what can it be? *(Soft music playing in the background.)*

Albert's spirit:
The music is pretty.

Gilda:
Yes, it is. Is this better *(Typewriter)* than the tablet? Let me know which is the better method; easier for you to move.

Albert's spirit:
Ok; at least we are trying. Let's practice a little bit each day; it will surprise us both.

Gilda:
How is the weather up there?

Albert's spirit:
Which weather?

Gilda:
The air that surrounds you in the Universe?

Albert's spirit:
It is light, not dense or heavy like your atmosphere. There are no respiratory illnesses. There are a few ailments that the spirits attached to earth feel; but it is all in their minds; they bring along their afflictions and apparently refuse to let them go; but all in time they dissipate. Time is a wonderful healer; not time like you measure, it's a different kind of measurement. One knows that things are flowing, moving along; it is an evolutionary process. Difficult, it's difficult for you to comprehend; in time you will know. I love all of you.

August 19, 2012.

Gabriel's spirit:

Peace and love dear sister; from the divine mountain we can see the real value of things; the small and tiny. You can see the huge ones in the distance; but enormous in moral courage, love, peace and charity.

So sister; climb the mountain, look at the distance, to put things in their place. Your eyes will assess and you will make good use of the time that you have left.

August 29, 2012.

Helena's spirit:

Peace and love sister dearest, it's been quite a while since we spoke last, but I'm always watching out for you; alert and caring for all of you. Quietly continue with your works, there are several more. You did well by joining the web radio. Nothing but nothing should give you anxiety; remain focused, follow your healthy and fertile intuition for the sake of serving. We wish you and the boys; clarity of thought, peace and health; illumination sister, equally for you and for the spirits.

August 30, 2012.

Albert's spirit:

Illumination and progress Gilda; not everything is dark, there is a light coming through the window; *"A slither of light"* indicating that there is an illuminated way for you; more things that you desire are coming; expect good news. It is not easy, we have told you, but it is gratifying to know that we are doing; not giving up; no, no, we energize, take a pause, and continue. That's all! We're never sitting around waiting for things to happen; you have to look for them, as you do daily; while asking for peace and understanding to go on searching; continue to write, the next book will be done. *(This book)* How? You will be guided; that's the formula; placed on the simple, plain, and loving road.

August 31, 2012.

Albert's spirit:

Everything can be beautiful when we look at it with lenses of love and optimism. When you give your respect and interest to the difficult, it becomes easier; a divine transformation occurs with love and interest. Peace, always in all hearts: closer to God with our thoughts and actions: nothing should divert us; we are cleaning up the debris from the road, by lifting stones; casting them aside. May everything be enlightenment, love and charity in our voyage. We are weak, but are strengthened daily by doing charity, in words, thoughts or actions. We are planting seeds along the way; which sometimes is twisted with inhumanity, but in our narrow path we sow, we deposit droplets of love.

September 1, 2012.

Gabriel's spirit:

Peace, peace, peace; we are many; there is much to tell. There is a long waiting list, and we seek the means to accelerate it. You always do your part and we will tell you how to do it better; there is a way; we seek the solution. Listen Gilda, good fortune is coming your way; safe and sound. It will happen with God's help, love, approval and mandate. We are many who wish to speak; we have important messages to share with our beloved ones.

September 3, 2012.

Unknown spirit:

Praise God in Heaven and all men of goodwill; I don't know what's happening to me, but I'm restless; there is something I should do. Peace and love sister... we'll have time.

Gilda:
Who said that?

Spirit:
Me; I am here; displeased.

Gilda:
I understand, but why? Tell me...

Spirit:
It is not for public consumption.

Gilda:
You can improve your situation with assistance, and you know it.

Spirit:
Yes; but I don't want to.

Gilda:
Why?

Spirit:
You already know.

Gilda:
Tell me.

Spirit:
Sans Souci

GIlda:
What's that?

Spirit:
A place

Gilda:
Where?

Spirit:
In Cuba

Gilda:
You came from there?

Spirit:
Yes.

Gilda:
Tell me what happened, and when?

Spirit:
Recently; well for you, a long ago.

Gilda:
Tell me the story.

Spirit:
It's too long and sad; nobody is interested.

Gilda:
On the contrary; it may be of interest to many and they are paying attention, wanting to help you. You'll be surprised by their reactions.

Spirit:
Do you think so?

Gilda:
I know it well. God loves us and listens to us; helping us always, always. So they say.

Spirit:
Who says?

Gilda:
A few here; listen to them. Are you there?

Spirit:
Yes, I'm still here.

Gilda:
Stay calm brother; take that hand that is extended to you. Have faith and be charitable to yourself. Go towards the light; until always.

September 4, 2012.

Albert's spirit;

My beloved Malena, I'm nearby as usual; to inspire and encourage you; waiting for our big day. Listen Gilda, everything passes by quickly, as I said; the hours vanish for you. Each one with their duties forgets and continues, that's all; don't give so much meaning to tomorrow; today always today. Keep in compliance and work; that will take you very far. On and on goes the ox carrying the load on its back; dreaming of the delicious food that awaits him; provided by his master. Concentrate, continue with your heavy cargo and you will achieve much.

September 5, 2012.

Unknown spirit:

Jesus, Joseph and Mary! I shouldn't speak to you, because you had me waiting for a long, long while; but I feel good doing it. We are friends for some time; meeting on a boat to the Americas, we became friends, good friends. I traveled with my family; you were going alone; everyone commented that it was very risky, that you were courageous. You were attractive but not beautiful, rather friendly and curious. You were looking for a better future and not looking for a boyfriend; you had left one behind. The years and centuries pass so quickly; they fly like thoughts. My name is Rosa; Rosita, I was called fondly. I was restless and inquisitive like you. We laughed and we were always asking in order to learn. A family in America was waiting for you; don't know who. I arrived ill with my parents, but I recovered soon. I worked as a seamstress in a theatre; in their wardrobe. We didn't see each other anymore. I remember you with much affection; until always.

Gabriel's spirit:

In the name of Almighty God; there is a lot to say, but calmly it will be done. Without confusion, nor mix-ups; simple and clear, so it will be. Life should not be so agitated, or convulsed I would say. Peace and love, sister; you're not the only one that suffers there are many like you, suffering. *"Caregivers"* patience saves them, as well as you. Hope drives them to go on day by day, with the same task, the same routine. Day in and day out! What's next? They wonder. Who knows? God knows.

Try to relax; your mind and emotions are drained; lack of recreation; as they say; in time rest will come. Let me say, you're still young at heart. Many pieces must be placed in their places; you'll do it slowly, very slowly, but firmly; therefore there must be an ending.

September 6, 2012.

Unknown Sprit:

Hey, are you through? Checking and double checking, goodness knows what. *(I was reviewing manuscripts.)* I was elderly when I passed on; died in a farm doing housework; I was a farmer's wife. We were decent, a good Christian family; going to church every Sunday. I don't remember what happened on the day I passed. It was my heart; never went to the doctor, didn't have the money; but, it wasn't bad at all; I just fell in the middle of the field on a sunny bright day and never woke up. That's pretty easy, don't you think? But then I woke up to see many smiling faces in a mist; a colored, mostly rosy vapor. Pink was my favorite color. I heard hymns, like the ones that we heard at church; I hummed along like I used to do. I couldn't carry a tune, you know.

My name was Doris, yes, it is a strange name, but it was for my grandmother's sake. We were of Scottish descent. I was fair skinned, tall, lanky, and not too attractive; but I had a nice smile and was well mannered. Hey, we will continue my story. It is important; don't chicken out; love and blessings to all; in the name of God.

September 7, 2012.

Helena's spirit:

Peace and love sister dear; although you have not heard me lately; I'm always very close by with my beloved Alberto, Monserrate and other members of our spiritual family, we walk together, supporting each other always; it is our joy and it will be yours in the future.

Doris' spirit;

Let me continue to tell you Gilda my life's story; I'm Doris. It's not dramatic or passionate, but ignorant; there are many like me; they work every day like puppets; they are robots of life. It is not evil, it is indifference; one can say it's the average person. It's something like some relatives of yours; they are not bad, but their comfort is of utmost importance always. The routine is sufficient; without making an effort not even to think. They just want pleasure even if it is so ephemeral; it doesn't matter how, or when. Yes, I had great love for God; I served my family and my church. We were farmers as I had said. We had a farm and comfort. My husband was a bit lazy but did his chores; just like my children; they were a little wild but they loved and respected me. Respect is very important in both worlds; I came to confirm it. My message is short, simple like me and sincere, also like me.

Do not be fooled with charities, prayers and walks on Sunday to the Church, if it's not in the heart of each one. I was attracted by what you were reading in your Gospel, about prayer; it has to come from the soul, the heart, and not from outside. When you arrive in this world of the spirit your soul is exposed; there are no covers or costumes; everything is as it is, and so you are accepted and placed; each one is in their place. Continue brothers and sisters, praying of course; the intention is everything. What do you ask for and why? Be benevolent and not selfish with your requests. We will soon do a little more. Thank you Father.

September 8, 2012.

Unknown spirit:

We all have our troubles, our moments of grief and sorrow; it is part of evolution and the tests. Remember that we came to this world to learn, amend and perfect; certainly enjoying the happy moments available at that level, but knowing that they are fleeting. The point is to recognize the moments of grief, and to buckle up and follow on rudder control, tracking toward our goals. Yes, it is easier said than done, but we understand and we will do it when needed. I really like this exercise!

Gabriel's spirit:

In the name of Almighty God; our brothers and sisters visit us unexpectedly; it is good that we can have the door open for good travelers who bring their baskets full of love and good advice. Welcome; Gilda, continue with Doris.

Doris' spirit:

Yes, I am very patient; it was my greatest virtue. Many came to me for advice. I thought about it a great deal, and then spoke; taking large pauses; it is my advice for today.

September 9, 2012.

Helena's spirit:

Good morning dearest sister, I come to tell you: that you have grown very much; as I told you in the past and I repeat; we are all proud of you. The day will come when we will show you how much, face to face; together in God's Glory. Nothing, you will lack nothing Gilda; you'll have whatever you need. Take advantage of this pretty day; prepare your soul for more feats; there will be a feast ready. Listen to this little sister; the tiredness will pass, your soul will shine with the joy of the good soldier honored with a medal from God; in this case, for your virtues, purpose, persistence and mercy.

September 10, 2012.

(As I read this message to my brother Nel: *(Also a medium.)* he received this spirit's name from his past life: *"Marco he was called; he just told me, and it was in Morocco, Africa."*)

Marco's spirit:

I want to begin this session, because I have so much to say. My name doesn't matter, since I've had so many names and monikers; but what's in my soul, that is what counts. I have suffered a lot, at length as they say; although I suffer no longer, thank God. I feel lighter and serene, but with a desire to talk, to comment, telling the world my story, because it is a pretty story. It does have some sad passages, but that happens to everyone at some point.

I don't remember when I started my journey on this planet Earth; centuries ago I believe; yes, hundreds of years ago, in a distant land of dust and forest; in primitive circumstances; strength prevailed; humans tyrannized each other for their needs; it was bestial I would say. There it begins, slowly deriving forces, and with a desire to progress, one takes a step forward almost always led by a hand from another soul that had advanced.

We stumble while we walk in the density; in a physical and spirit cloud, but a ray of light, although small, could be seen. We know that there is something beyond, and we are still searching for that light that promises so much; that is the birth of faith. It is a very interesting picture, because soon we crawled on and we dragged on, but as good soldiers, we tried to pick ourselves up; wanting to walk on our own feet; stumbling and falling, but motivated by the innate hope, placed there by the Creator Father. All that process is very slow and painful at times, but it is growth anyway. The road is in sight and we arrived at another life experience; other circumstances, other clothing and mentality; we are another, but we are the same; it is difficult to explain. Then there we notice some familiar souls, that more or less, began this journey along with us; from the same neighborhood you could say; unmixed we recognize each other and that made us happy. We continue doing our utmost, even if very little, to exist in this new environment, which is less bad than the previous one, but still tempestuous and difficult. It's an upward step; we take breaks to breath and regain strength, but the small steps taken are heavy. We learn a little, yes, you learn from others that live there, in that strange place; still not knowing our span of progress; or the Earth time that had elapsed. There is a slight disorientation but we preserved the ardent desire; with more firmness and clarity of purpose to get ahead.

There are power outages; physical life stops in those pauses and we float in the universe entertained with its beauty. There we find familiar faces, urging us, encouraging us and cheering us on that realm. Soon the lights come around again, transporting us to other new earthly places. There we are strangers, but with others known from the past; without realizing it we joined them and we understood that there was a reason for all this. It is an effect with a cause; a motive for our new home. We will continue soon; peace sister, thank you Father.

September 12, 2012.

Helena's spirit: *(At lake)*

Dearest sister Gilda, yes, more waiting; but this peaceful site does you so much good; your soul rejoices with nature; its beauty encourages and refreshes you. Calmly continue your work; what you read in the Gospel is very true; courage is needed to face the world and their disbelief. You need great faith to raise a white flag that says eternal life, eternal love, eternal God. The most important part will come; the story of a family of spirits: *"Spiritual ecstasy."*

September 13, 2012.

Unknown spirit:

Oh my goodness; here I am again! Thank God that we can communicate; that is truly a blessing. Let's see, my message is rather simple, I am a simple soul.

With much love to share; I have been given a *"reprieve"* because of my love and dedication. We are all on the same page, as they say.

Gosh, let's see, I hate interruptions, because I lose my train of thought. Life here is so special; yes, that is want I wish to say. My life here is pretty, very pretty; because I wish it to be pretty. We make it as we wish; that is the way it works. We use all our resources; mental, imaginative, emotional, with our experiences, and we create our new home; painted with our thoughts and wishes. It can be done by a few working together; like a community, each one doing their part; creating details for that home. It's like a physical house, painting, decorating it; each member adds details to brighten it up; making it pretty, just like what I said. But we must also clean the house; like on earth. We must keep our home neat, tidy; all with our thoughts. There must be peace and harmony amongst all, in order to maintain a solid structure. I want you to know that we welcome visitors invited by the members of the family.

In our world there are spirit enterprises similar to the earthly ones. The souls sing, work, study and pray; there is also joy, peace, fortitude, enthusiasm and persistence. The entities are delighted with what they see; but in other cases it can be the contrary. God we love you; it's so important to love God, to love thy self; to love all; it makes all the difference. The colors are brighter; the day is prettier, surroundings look better, the picture changes with love. Everything is difficult when hate surrounds us; hate is outrages, it's like the black plaque. The antidote is love and peace, mixed with a touch of cheer. Drink it little sister, savor it and pick yourself up. The party is just beginning.

September 15, 2012.

(My books; Wings Mystical / Mystical Wings, were published.) (At the lake)

Gabriel's spirit:

We are happy, very happy; jubilant with the events. We know good things are getting closer all gifts from Monserrate's pretty precious God. Your mom is happy because she knows that you're in pursuit of something greater; larger and more important; it is the happiness of our brothers on Earth. Yes, yes, it's a nice day; the breeze caresses you, the Sun and the clearness. May you have harmony to think, meditate, and enjoy all of God's blessings. It's beautiful to have faith, to work and to feel personal satisfaction; you see the rewards from God with your children; you see positive results; thank you Father for the many gifts.

September 19, 2012.

Gabriel's spirit: *(At lake)*

In the name of Almighty God; not everyone can be exemplary because we have so many faults, but if we make an effort, faults can be lessened, diminished and even corrected. That is very possible but it depends on each one of us and what we seek and whatever our souls, tired of suffering and erring hold dear. There's always, always hope; the possibility is always there; It presents itself, and returns; there are many opportunities to redeem ourselves; we only lack willpower. Little Gilda is now a full fledge woman; therefore no more tripping, or nonsense, or tantrums; no, nothing of the sort.

Let's put aside, discord and whims; seeking only peace in our souls and contemplating only what's of value to God. Continue your redeeming journey sister; you will know when to take flight. One more day struggling and of growth; thus is incarnation; although apparently not, it's helpful. We notice mild, subtle changes, indicating progress, and that fills us with joy because we know that we have not wasted our time, that we have made good use of every moment to amend and advance, as we so desired. Who hasn't sinned according to the world? But we learn, we learn. It is very sad to make the same mistakes, over and over; repeating the same nonsense as in childhood, blaming others and the circumstances. We must forget the past, whatever it was; it is gone.

Today is the result of yesterday; today we are another, because of a yesterday that we left behind. We are blessed if we can look back and see our poorly directed footprints; knowing that now our feet are placed on a solid foundation. If you have reached that stage; rejoice and celebrate your birthday. Happy Birthday Gilda, from all of us.

Unknown spirit:

Praise the Virgin Mother; I'm a very good Catholic; a believer, I love God above all things. I love you, sister; and I want to help you; you have done much with your limited knowledge. Do not be afraid of anything and no one. Everything passes by quickly; even the strength and unruliness; slipping away as the sometimes agitated breeze. We are looking for peace and quiet in our souls. I have spoken!

October 7, 2012.   *(At lake)*

(I was watching a newborn duckling swimming alone from one side of the lake to the other; I thought: what is that very small duckling searching for while leaving behind his mother and his siblings?)

Unknown spirit:

Every creature has intelligence, although sometimes tiny; everything is in a scale. Everyone searches for their well-being, their improvement, calming concerns; it's the law of nature. Some quicker than others, some friendly, others indifferent, but all are one, with the same raw materials; with a divine spark; God in its interior, ignited to illuminate at times. Burning in its evolution; warming each other, sharing the light. It is a fraternity of beings united by a love, but unknown by many. That love can be very small, negligible; a little spark nothing more, unknown by the carrier, but it's there; God given when created; though this is unrecognized or not asked for; it is there, waiting to grow and shine. Sooner or later the brightness will increase; guiding all towards their Universal heritage.

Gabriel's spirit:

In the name of Almighty God; yes, there are calmness and peace here; and with you sister. Maintain your spiritual posture; *"Whatever it takes."* There are always some gaps in the road, but we have learned to maneuver around them, thus not interrupting our trip. Sister, there is gratitude in thee also in us. Let me tell you that our experiences with you are very refreshing.

October 24, 2012.

Unknown spirit:

Peace and love dear Gilda; I was waiting for you; sometimes you're slow; it is the years, they do count; but you're spirit is brimming; full of health and youth. Listen; I've come from far away, looking for souls, alleviating them when they ask for help.

I am a happy and satisfied guardian: I am your **Guardian Angel**. I've also suffered very much with you, because of your ordeals and disorders; but you've straightened out, although there is still some more to do. Please, believe what I say; everything is possible with God's permission; I repeat. Jesus loves you and your children; the Virgin loves you and your sons and brother, all of you: as Gabriel; that is your guide: says: all is done in the name of God.

October 31, 2012.

Gabriel's spirit:

In the name of Almighty God; you know well Gilda dear that everything has a cause; but you must always take a look at the root, no matter how many years or centuries have elapsed. Not today or tomorrow, but always; our love and devotion are like that, and it is motivating, making us very happy.

Let me tell you a very beautiful and ancient story; it is about a hardworking woman who lived in the Far East, many centuries ago. She was beautiful but reckless, arrogant, cocky and abusive; all these faults she had; but within, she felt goodness and a desire to share, and did it with a reduced circle of followers and family members who had her sympathy. This story contains very much symbolism and answers some questions; unknown to you and to the other players involved; it has a long list of characters and a swirl of passions.

When this middle-aged woman passed on, and upon awakening in the spirit world, she found herself, devastated, sad and fearful; she didn't know what to expect, or where to turn. Her weak voice brought no assistance, but suddenly she saw a group of souls approaching and muttering. What were they looking for and saying? She wondered; feeling alive, not realizing her disembodied state; because she was a very materialistic spirit. The entities came closer and in unison spoke as if it were an echo vibrating; the sound resounded in her ears. *"Rise up and walk, thus said our Master Jesus, do it."* She rose slowly and paid attention to what the entities with blinking lights said as they surrounded her. *"You must return to Earth many times to pay off your debt of indifference. Our Father has given you abundance; a comfortable life, and possibilities of doing substantial charitable works, but you wasted it. Unfortunately even now, you do not recognize your errors of judgment. The sadness in the future will make you reflect and reach conclusions about your goals in the terrestrial world. Tears or cries are worthless, only strong hard work and constant determination, will help your cause. You're not wicked, you have succumbed to the passions and they ruined you. Rise from your human misery, and go on toward your new duties. You will have new goals and purposes of assistance to the world. Over the centuries you will achieve your goals, and you will celebrate this meeting with your brothers that love you. Go in peace, and comply."*

November 2, 2012.

Gabriel's spirit:

In the name of Almighty God; without God there is nothing. Let us continue the sad story of this creature in pain. Evil does not mean indifference; evil is doing harm to others; but this is not the case. Lack of love is selfishness, its indifference; attachment to the physical passions, to the pleasures of the flesh, regardless of the consequences. They are extremes in the sensual appetites; it's the desire for comfort based on the sacrifices of others; all that is lack of love. To avoid seeing the pain in others and not caring, it is not evil it is indifference; lack of compassion. We must be very clear, about what our goals are and about our commitments with ourselves and with others; here and there. We are unified, we are all one; we do to one and we do it to all the others.

"The Dead Sea", is the location where the events of this sad and meaningful story took place. *"The Dead Sea"* I would say the dead inhabitants; thrashing each other in a stampede of sensual pleasure. No respite from earthly whims and torments; all arousing havoc.

Another unknown spirit:

Let me continue; because I was part of that barrage of soulless bodies, scrambling for pleasures and satisfactions, unknown even now to mankind. Deadly sins that brought misery to the Earth; I am not exaggerating, nor fantasying; I want to clean my slate and start fresh. That is what I always felt down deep in my heart, because I didn't think that I had a soul, I just felt the body; I didn't believe that we had anything else; how tragic and how sad.

The mechanical movements of the body guided us, like robots; while feeling lifeless. Until one awesome moment of spirit revitalization, I would say; a jolt from the sky, occurred; a shaking of the earth; a stirring of the seas. We all ran to save ourselves, from a tremendous earthquake and tsunami. Quickly running desperately to the caves in the mountains; huddling in the dark; trembling with fear and uncertainty; with difficulty breathing in the hot moisture filled caverns.

I lost consciousness and saw myself floating, up, up to the top of the cave and through the rocks, and then suddenly cradled by invisible unknown arms that rocked me; with a secure and soft feeling surrounding me. It was a wonderful emotion; love at last! Unknown to me; love! Gratitude sprung from me for the first time in my life. Unknown to all, devastation was occurring few were left; I was one of them. We will continue, with God's permission and help.

November 5, 2012.

Unknown spirit:

Peace and love, light and progress, Gilda; we continue with our story. The night was very long, so seemed to her, while waiting for news of her future. The wait brought desperation and a feeling of being trapped; but the sun always rises; no matter the duration of the night. So it happens to us all; but dawn brings hope and mental agility to make decisions and take the reins in the matter. We cannot shrink, but we must grow in understanding and faith in order to make the necessary determinations. With hope the light always shines in the darkness; faith brings hope and allows enlightenment to open the pathway of love and understanding.

Let's get back to the young woman delirious with her tragedy, her dissatisfaction and indifference. We have repeated that the only solution is to fulfill what we have promised.

Another unknown spirit;

Let me tell you sister, my version of the story; I was close, very close, to that rebellious woman, that wasn't evil. I saw the events; they were turbulent, but long, strong and firm steps were taken. Not everything is negative in this narrative; there is goodness and huge triumphs. There are many interesting characters; one is your current father who was Asian; with a dictator's mind set; in behavior and in process. He always came up on top and still has not lost the custom, even now after so many centuries of suffering. His evolution has been very slow, but God has given him many blessings.

It is laziness and sluggishness, instead of evil. He doesn't like discomfort; his welfare always comes first; it is his motto. Unfortunately you had him as family; he was your father then. Your rebellion towards him was born then, in that distant Asian land, because he was tyrannical and abusive. We will continue, always in the name of God. Light and progress, Gilda, stay calm; continue with a slow step, sure and firm; with spiritual stability. Your Inspiration will continue, and you'll write the next book *(This book)* in God's name.

November 11, 2012.

Albert's spirit:

Peace and love always, for ever and ever; united by an unwavering love; lucky us that we feel this emotion so pure and solid, blessed by God. Nothing, nothing confuses us; nothing makes us hesitate; on the contrary with more resistance, the stronger we are. Absolute tranquility is essential for your work; look for it and don't lose it.

November 16, 2012.

Gabriel's spirit:

In the name of Almighty God; God's peace be with you, dearest sister. Fear nothing, on the contrary, stay confident and calm in your redeeming march. More discipline Gilda; no sadness, just joy in your pampered little girl soul. You'll see what beautiful results you'll have; the books will have wings; they will fly alone. Trust our Father; He is your best promoter. We know nothing; we are so tiny, and we believe we're big and powerful, but we are microscopic. God puts us in our place frequently, and it's necessary, so as to learn His power and nature's. *(A storm hit NYC.)* God is Immense, Wise, Fair and Generous; we must obey him, not out of fear; but with love and respect; knowing that he loves us and wants the best for us. The Creator assists with our losses and our sorrows; let us give thanks, now and forever.

November 21, 2012.

Unknown spirit:

Let's see! What will be, will be, is often said; but it's not necessarily so. There are means to rectify, to correct and mend; situations that can lead to other conclusions, thus ending the conditions that can seem unavoidable. Watch your next step, that's true, but also watch the pace of your step. Take a pause and then take a step; therefore avoiding a mishap. We rush; snap to it. Why? Take the needed pause to reflect. You are often inspired, enlightened, guided and saved by guardian angels or God's messengers. Oh yes, it happens more often than you think. So let's get down to the basics: Stop and calm yourself, ask for assistance in the form of inspiration or otherwise, wait patiently for it, because it always arrives. Understand, reflect, and determine the right cause of action to take. Do it; and thank God and His helpers.

Happiness on planet Earth is ephemeral; it doesn't exist completely. Our good acts are the base, and it can be solid or it can crumble; everything depending on us. Let's make our lives a temple to God; full of beautiful flowers, which are our pure and loving thoughts.

November 22, 2012.

(Thanksgiving Day)

Gabriel's spirit:

In the name of Almighty God; love for you Gilda, from all of us. Thank you for the flowers; symbol of your love; there is always a radiant glow in your soul;

peacefully guiding your steps. Yes, yes, Happy Thanksgiving! Let's Praise God for allowing us to communicate; love compels us to do beautiful things; it's as crystal water blessed by Him. May God's peace reign here, now and always. Monserrate, Helena and Albert are here; all hugging you. *(My hands rose up automatically and began to applaud; like if the spirits were applauding me.)*

December 8, 2012.

Gabriel's spirit:

The House is full of joy and hope. Gilda, believe it, all is harmony and balance in the Universe, as it should be here. Look for the light of reason sister; calming yourself you will find it. The breeze will lift you in your desire to do. The cycles come and go; so our spiritual lives pass by quickly, although in human time they seem to crawl. We sense the changes; go along with your intuition. There is no reason to worry, only search for God's light, which shines best.

December 17, 2012.

Gabriel's spirit: *(Lake)*

In the name of Almighty God; there is nothing better than tranquility; the environment influences our dispositions. Nature is our best escape from anguish or sorrow; not alcohol, nor drugs or other passions.

The serenity and peacefulness of the sounds and the natural landscape; flowers, birds, lakes and springs; all that is God; His love and harmony are present in everything, rocking us, calming, loving us.

Blessed are those who live near or surrounded by nature, with less concrete and more foundations.

December 19, 2012.

Helena spirit;

Dearest sister, none of us are exemplary or virtuous; not one of us, but we aspire to something better; whether it be spiritual, mental or material. We must try to advance morally above all things. We are identified by our acts, actions, words and feelings; they are our business cards to the world. Others judge and classify us by those elements and by our appearances. Each one reading another; it is a constant survey among all; whether or not our capabilities or expectations seem to other people as pleasant or positive, it affects us. Human beings respond; they support and help by the impressions received in that spontaneous invisible survey, but perceived by everyone. We go through life showing our soul or spirit that expands or retracts according to our thoughts, intentions and feelings. It's a portrait of our soul, which the world contemplates.

January 2, 2013.

Gabriel's spirit:

Preserve your peace; it is your lantern. With peace, you can think better, you can see better and work better. That torch of love that is God lives in each one, and no matter how much the winds blow; it will never shut it off; not ever. You just have to search within, listening to your inner voice; you're little voice warning you, guiding you, encouraging you.

Be attentive and you will hear it, follow its wise indications, leading you towards a portal; opening for you a large window to the world.

January 3, 2013.

Gabriel's spirit:

Your artistic career had reached a crossroads, and with spiritual inspiration, divine assistance, and with maternal support you finally found the path of light; the honorable path of service to humanity. Few have the great opportunity and responsibility to perform such a task. When entering a point of emancipation, the spirit looks for a way to share knowledge that ignites; wakes up the sleepy and exhausted brains; from living erroneously. Yes, the task is huge and heavy, but necessary and possible. Only needed are spiritual strength and human determination. With compassion we must awaken them; shaking their minds, splashing their bewildered souls, so they may take advantage of their stay in this inhospitable world.

January 4, 2013.

Unknown spirit:

We must define ourselves in life; to be or not to be? That is the repeated universal question; to believe or not to believe? But not a weak belief, nor a semi incredulous belief; no, no, a belief with firmness and jubilation. Believe in what? That is the big question. First and most important is to believe in God; a Supreme Creative Intelligence, Wise and Benevolent. We must love and respect God; the Universal Life Force that drives us.

You ask: why? I answer; because it is the explanation to all your doubts. The answer to the incessant question: why am I here? For what, what do I seek? There is a cause, a purpose in all this; in your life. Religions, doctrines and philosophies established by humans leave you fearful, empty. Their litanies and prayers are gone with the wind; repeated without sense or passion. The rituals and rules make you cringe, baffling you. The best and true religion is in you; in your soul, in your spirit and in your connection with the Creator; together at work for Universal goodness. Each human being is connected, linked; all loved by the Supreme Creator; search for it; it is there, in you.

January 5, 2013.

Gabriel's spirit:

God is everything! He is our Creator! We are his creation; it is as simple as that. We are all learning little by little; some faster, others slower or are lazy; but here we are together; each one looking forward, to growth in spirit. Some aware of this truth; others entertained, distracted with life's rhythm. We the spirit messengers are indebted to that Omnipotent Father, because at some point we were stupid or lazy and failed more than once; but encouraged by our brothers in spirit; we recovered consciousness, lifting ourselves from the human dust, to help suffering humankind. Everything is possible when there is a will; *"To will, is power"* repeat the spirit advisors; you can still achieve it, if you really want it; you're still on time.

January 6, 2013.

Gabriel's spirit:

Features of goodness are in you; many expectations and dreams; you've always had them; but also inconsistencies, shyness, that have been obstructions. All of that is part of growth; and that's why we're here; not to waste time, and not only to have fun; although God does want our happiness, but well deserved. We must struggle and suffer to surpass; overcoming obstacles. There's no straight or easy path in that world. Greetings sister Gilda; don't collapse with the daily, sometimes boring routine. They are solid and firm steps that day by day you take; at times dragging yourself while distressed. You're carrying the sadness in your soul, of the captive who wants forgiveness and its liberation. Routine deteriorates the soul and body; we know it. But the laborious and believing spirit, doesn't succumb; it toughens.

January 7, 2013.

Gabriel's spirit:

We don't know very much little sister; we are all learning; crawling with our lessons: but someday we will all reach our goal, whatever and wherever. Let put aside the sorrows, the conflicts, the contests, yes the challenges; we are not competing; no, we are unified supporting each other. The strong helping the weak; holding each other up with the weaknesses that we all have. What is better than too feel the support and affection of a brother, knowing that you do not succumb because you're held up while you learn to walk; it is so, sister. I ask for enlightenment from God for each one; igniting brains abused and mutilated by setbacks; it is a loving light that heals all the souls hurt by human indifference. Glory to God!

January 9, 2013.

Helena's spirit:

Peace and love sister dearest; the lights are always lit on the road of love. On that straight road illuminated with the love of God we will never deviate or get lost, nor will we suffer accidents. Pretty things are in the inkwell for you little sister; soaring, with increased transmissions to support you. An ignited lamp in the night is your life; good soul. You're waking up from your slumber, with the Sun appearing in the path; it's a lovely picture. Expect the events that are developing. It is not tame water, but wild sea waves that are at your door in the distance. Multiple paths will open up, adorned with turquoise crystal like quartz; which repudiates the negative and attracts the positive. Magnetic energies will encourage you to continue and conclude your goal. There is a feast, tasty and abundant; ready to serve. You will see results.

January 17, 2013.

Helena's spirit:

Beloved sister, we feel joyful, seeing you so devoted, so resigned. It has been and still is a slow road with grief, tears, doubts and unanswered questions. All that has trained you for your current work: receiver, writer and communicator; spreading love seeds, our seeds of love. Consistency is important in everything; discipline and action go hand in hand; that is the winning formula.

Many things will present themselves all together; like the banquet that you were informed; but tasty, with succulent dishes; that are your great works.

January 20, 2013.

Gabriel's spirit:

We can all do much more; it's within our reach. The problem is laziness, indifference and dissatisfaction with life. Many waste their time, with laments and, complaints; rebelling against their circumstances. They are rabbits trapped in their own mud; it's quicksand that sucks them in, when they want to get out of the well. That is why we must break bad habits; those patterns of harmful conduct from childhood; sometimes just by copying our parents. They are the moaners, unhappy; squirming; not knowing why.

Let's leave aside that sad picture, and look at the joy of living, with a fervent hope in the soul, with an optimistic and happy heart; that even though you suffer, you don't see it as an obstacle to go forward and get out of the pit; by knowing that we are able with our own interests, caution and purposes; to finally manage to install ourselves in that great site; pleased, comfortable and delighted.

January 24, 2013.

Albert's spirit:

Understanding that man does not live by bread alone; spirituality is needed; and a lot of it, in that dense, heavy and hostile world; you know buoyancy of the soul helps the body. Everyone can achieve much; it all depends on the attitude of each one.

What are the common goals that unify us? What are the purposes of each one? There are so many ingredients in the mixture to give it good seasoning; it's like a stew with a few cooks. We know and do not know; we are in between this and that; such is life; but even without knowing, it's our obligation to continue struggling, learning and working; it is the eternal commitment; knowing that God loves us, and that we are spirits in evolution; and we also know that we love and we are loved. Those are all good and positive things, and with that, it is sufficient for us.

January 28, 2013.

(Reading "Posthumous Works" by Allan Kardec.)

Gabriel's spirit:

Peace and love, Gilda; those are interesting passages that illustrate the importance of human thought and the will of the spirit. We are capable of much but many mutilate themselves every day, with petty, silly and selfish thoughts; thus drowning in a fountain of disaffection. Gilda, you can see the world as it is, and that you have lived in the flesh; many years of ignorance, anxiety and sleeplessness; now you finally awaken, wishing to regain lost time; although you are aware of rescuing several works that you had pending. Let's discard hopelessness, laziness, indifference, and all that is harmful. Discard whatever poisons the spirit; affecting the body; a victim of human beings harmful appetites.

February 4, 2013.

Gabriel's spirit:

There are many souls who come to the terrestrial world with many concerns; they are happy because they dream awake, but they also stumble and hurt themselves in their hectic rush wanting to do. So it has been with you, sister; you've now calmed down at last; taking the necessary pauses; reflecting, enjoying small moments of stillness, satisfied with your good deeds. New tasks you will have and joyful you will feel; sacred commitments you will finalize. It has been a long rosary; at the beginning a litany; now recited with joy.

The music is filtering through your window and you will hear divine harmonies. The end of the road nears, and happily you will return home.

February 7, 2013.

Gabriel's spirit:

In the name of Almighty God; hello Gilda, good girl; with the particulars about your flowers and the care of the plants, you are saying *"I love life"* despite the suffering and blunders. Each cycle is charming so you must rescue the charm; show it well and enjoy it. Gilda, it's magnificent to learn and to be able to pass it on to others who are in great need; without knowing how and where to find assistance, guidance and training. Let us all march onward toward the towering hills, with our backpacks filled, crammed; heavy with the many lessons in golden books that we carry to those who aspire. There is much to say, a lot. It is a good time to spread the grain with the benevolent wind that comes from God.

These fertile seeds will grow in time, in the fertile ground of suffering humanity; regenerating their souls and bodies. There will be no obstacle; the roads will open. Go on sister, with your works; many they are, and will be, until your glorious and harmonious departure No more crying; only plenty of delight and jubilation.

February 12, 2013.

Unknown spirit:

We spirits are affected seeing so much ingratitude on Earth. The world is devastated by iniquity; Indifference and selfishness reigns among the masses who are entertained. We ask ourselves: how can we reach them? How can we touch them and spiritualize them? Making them reconsider; so they can change their ways; moving, pushing to one side of the crowd, looking for the light. It is an arduous task; many try to impact, without results.

February 15, 2013,

Gabriel's spirit: *(On the Lake.)*

In the name of Almighty God, dearest Gilda; surprises and more surprises will come from here and there. Such is life; the sower throws the seeds with great love and sacrifice and unexpectedly sees the harvest; the multicolored flowers and delicious fruits growing. How not to believe in God? Says Monserrate; about her adored dearest God; that has helped and helps each one so much, every day. The good thing about this site *(Lake)* is the peace and privacy; ideal for the writer.

February 16, 2013.

Monserrate's spirit;   *(My mom)*

God loves us Gilda, Praise God; Father thank you for so much joy. The New Orleans idea is well thought out, perfect; *(I traveled to Louisiana and researched mom's past lifetime there.)* a small book will come; Albert will help you. You were there to pick up seeds of the past that are still living and vibrating. You will find information step by step, of the beautiful and successful stories of souls, who loved and respected each other.

February 19, 2013.

Gabriel's spirit:

In the name of Almighty God; dear Gilda, the cargo is heavy but yet light, due to faith that moves mountains. There are no obstacles for faith; with it the burdens are weightless. We all desire easy, quick and simple answers, but it's not possible; sometimes, and in some cases responses are slow because of circumstances. Clarity of thought and soul are necessary, attached to that solid faith all the time.

We are your brothers and allies, very unified; looking for new goals. We cannot leave behind any task or service because our commitment with God and with ourselves is irrevocable. There's no doubt that there are stumbling blocks but they are of the material world and are worthless; they pass and are small, we deal with them; overcoming them. Let me tell you Gilda, the ideal would be a wagon to help you carry the cargo for long distances. We, your invisible allies are the wagon.

February 22, 2013.

Gabriel's spirit:

In the name of God Almighty; we all come to embrace you, to give you our cosmic energy. Yes, it is me; Gabriel. There is nothing better than peace in the soul, at home and in the world. We all have a duty to contribute to world peace with our personal peace. They are drops that are deposited in the same sea. We want to encourage you little sister, to go on in peace, with your active, firm and constant devotion. You do not stop, that is you; tireless with your sacred responsibilities. The new book is developing and beautiful nuances it will have; some lovely and interesting stories are still missing. How can there be those who doubt? All around, they can see the wisdom and mercy of the Creator; the harmony of the Universe is a noticeable, palpable sign of a Supreme Intelligence. Many humans are cocky, self-satisfied and ungrateful, not to recognize a universal cosmic energy in control of everything.

February 23, 2013.

Gabriel's spirit:

In the name of Almighty God: we are going to write, even if it's not much. Explore and clean up; not everyone can do it; it's too much of an effort. They don't have the will and much less the desire. It's easier to continue in the same manner; without altered morals. We are always asking for illumination, because that terrestrial plane is in shadows; with dark clouds of discontent. Many rays of light are needed to penetrate the fog. What for? That's the motto of laziness; however, they request assistance from God daily; and with what right? Where are the good examples? Where's the proof? The behavior remains the same! Don't ask for anything, if you can't give in return!

February 25, 2013.

Albert's spirit:

Peace and love dearest Gilda, It's me Albert; there are many of us here; a brother is waiting to continue his story. We will achieve our dream of total automatic writing, you'll see; let's continue practicing, like now. You must finish this work, because there will be a small pause; "a breather for you." I love you.

Urack's spirit:

Yes, as I said, my determination was to love and it is ironic, that I felt it more deeply after the devastation. At that remote time human beings were bestial, with no thoughts or feelings; similar to many humans now. Only survival concerned them, but those cataclysmic events put them in their small place, compared with one major force; that we know it's our Creator; it was incomprehensible to them that something stronger and unknown existed. Now we were gradually learning to think although they were vague ideas; but questions arose, and thus consciousness unfolded. These are very ancient memories, memorable because they were the catalyst calming a thirst for progress, and pushing us towards our destiny, in the name of God.

February 26, 2013.

Gabriel's spirit:

In the name of Almighty God; we never know where the surprises come from, but they come. That's one of God's good things: He always gives us gifts. They are manifestations of a Father who pampers us and we are awarded for our behavior; yes, yes, as with children; that we are. We want to give you gifts sister, you know well that we do it with inspiration.

Urack's spirit:

The rains came and went; we were all homeless: many slept and slept with depressions; slowly dying. Only the very strong survived; I was young, strong and very determined to live. I went ahead; in search of survival in any way or form; and I also felt a wave of something that I had not felt before; it was a spark placed there by God; a renaissance unknown to me, because I was still a wild creature. On the road to nowhere, some stragglers met up with us; they were survivors like me, strong men and women; there were no children. We stayed close together for protection; hearing animal noises, apparently looking for food; just like us. Scattered herbs and fruits kept us alive.

I continued to feel new sensations; although I knew nothing about emotions; I had never really felt anything but passions of the flesh. Now for the first time I was concerned about another; a woman that traveled with us. It was not the usual feeling of lust or self-gratification; it was more a sense of caring; a wanting to protect her. I liked the feeling and it reminded me of the unknown arms that cuddled me after the cataclysm. At last God had awakened my consciousness with His tender love; we are all created with a conscience and free will, but it was just dormant. You ask; where am I going with all this? Well episodes like mine are still happening now; although the earth has progressed. Yes, there are still many savages like me; with dormant consciousness, hearts and souls. They inhabit that planet, and they must be shaken to the core, in order to feel God's love within. Words do not reach them easily, because they are so distracted; but at certain time their loneliness and personal dissatisfaction is enormous, feeling an immense void; a missing link to the Creator; knowing something must change; asking, how? Is it possible to find sincere warmth and tenderness in that world of make believe? It is a carnival of sensual fantasies mixed with materialism and the love of money. They choke with their consumer cocktail, and when the materialistic high fades, the soul shrieks and laments its deception; they had believed everything was perfect.

Back to my story: the woman, reciprocated, but I was also baffled by my civil conduct, because usually I was a brute. Communicating in a very minimal way, but an understanding was reached, that she would be my companion. Hardly speaking we kept on traveling; until reaching a washed out settlement that still had some rustic adobe structures standing. We called it home; the climate had change for the better and we believed that we could live there for a while. My name was Urack; this land was near the Persian Sea, centuries ago. My story in part is unpleasant and yet enticing. We will continue.

February 27, 2013.

Gabriel's spirit;

In the name of Almighty God: thank you Father for so much joy; we understand and appreciate the many blessings we have received. There is much to be done and we do not stop to contemplate the difficulty of the task we have undertaken; we only march on with a strong and solid faith towards the culmination of our work. The barn is full of good seeds; we must scatter them in fertile soil; knowing it or not, the benefitted. Sister dear, surprises will come floating through the air; beneficial thoughts from the enlightened entities, streaming through your window; they are whispers of love and peace, exalting your spirit, slightly tired from so much work. God with His benevolence sends his assistants with missions of support to our brothers and sisters on Earth.

Urack's spirit:

There was no cowardice or hesitation; only an insistence in advancing, to know more and more, about that new unknown light that illuminated the way. Now we were many; united by the misfortune that had been a teacher for our primitive and naive souls. Time was flying as we pushed and sped to reach who knows where. Finally reaching an ancient civilization with greater advancement and intelligent humans; it was Atlantis; but we found ourselves in a desolate area; at the end of the peninsula. The other part, it was said; was advanced and progressive; in all senses. We were fish out of the water; but we knew that for some reason we had survived. I had become a leader. Up to here, sister; peace.

March 3, 2013.

Gabriel's spirit:

In the name of Almighty God; congratulating you once again Gilda; your perseverance is admirable. There is nothing that stands in our way; quickly we do and publish our loving and wise words. God is very generous to everyone; you realize it at all times; we thank thee Father.

Urack's spirit:

Praise God! Let me go on with my story. Days and months went by of our odyssey; finally we set up in the beautiful Atlantis; in the outskirts of the resplendent city. Restricted when we arrived, but the prosperity surrounding us provided the means to thrive. The group held together; we were a large family united by misfortune, but we respected each other because we were victorious over destruction and chaos.

My wife had a son, very similar to me, strong and bold; and sweet like his mother. Tremors were felt in the distance; the inhabitants feared another cataclysm. Everyone knew our history; villages disappeared, with scattered residents. We did not know what could happen; so we just lived day by day. The native inhabitants of the city were majestic, well-liked, intelligent and benevolent. They asked us to join their society; although we were not very attractive and our customs were primitive and uncivilized, and we were naive; like lost children with a desire to learn.

March 4, 2013.

Urack"s spirit:

Praise God in Heaven and all souls of goodwill; we are gathered here, praying with you; giving thanks for so many blessings. There is no doubt, fear or hesitation; we just believe and work on His behalf. We are very happy, hopeful and ready to continue our stories with God's harmony. Not a day went by, in which someone didn't ask how we got there; going from nothing to opulence; so drastic was the change. We experienced a fast spirit growth that we knew had to be a major force that protected us; there was a reason for this. Faith was the great treasure; it kept us composed, standing and serene. What would happen? It was the perpetual question in our thoughts; and it had to happen after many years; I was already an old man, like my faithful wife. The trumpets sounded in warning of alarm; as alerts in the night. The earth trembled and the waters boiled; the lack of control was total; again residents ran in panic, screaming; lightning rained down upon the Earth; multitudes of terrified souls disappeared. For all of us it was a bitter repetition of our nightmare; we sought to escape but there was none; the waters wrapped everything.

March 5, 2013.

(I had a dispute and was feeling upset; for a moment I lost the serenity needed to do my prayers.)

Gabriel's spirit: *(Lake)*

Don't let anyone get you down; good sister. Your work is the priority; not you and not him. You are simply a vehicle with imperfections, as your car is for you.

Use it well, take care of it, drive it, but don't crash it. Stillness is essential for inspiration; the mental and spiritual channels open up with the silence of nature. Reflect; that calmness is very much needed.

March 6, 2013.

Unknown spirit:

Oh my God! It is wonderful that we can write; thank you Jesus! Tell me little sister, how do you do it? But you do it. I am your friend from way back when; as they say; we always loved and helped each other. I want to tell you what happened to me: please write.

It will help a few. I know that you have someone else pending, but give me a few minutes. I was a rebel like you; oh yes, also very domineering like you; that is why we got along so well. I learned my lesson the hard way; again just like you. I have reincarnated a few times since then; in the distant Argentina; were we lived a couple of times. There I started my purgatory; I had to sacrifice family and home in order to repent; and I have. Lessons must be learned, sooner or later, better sooner than later. God is merciful he reads our regret and aids us when we cry out for help. I have come today to add my limited wisdom to your notes; I enjoyed your friendship and now I wanted to be a part of this work; thank you dear friend and as you say frequently; mostly thank God. My message is so simple; there is hope for all; always; but there has to be sincere remorse; a true desire to make good, to rectify deeds. We are not evil; just misguided and spoiled rotten. Our best friend is God; our buddies are his messengers; together they assist; lifting us up from the earth's pit.

Don't stray from our Creator; I just wanted to say that. God bless you, your men and the little girl; dear friend, see you soon. Mildred.

March 7, 2013.

Urack's spirit:

Light and progress Gilda; let's continue; we must not ponder so much on details, but in the great teachings; in the many lessons in our stories. We are students and every step taken teaches us how to walk on the narrow straight road to God. I am Urack; as I said; we were a herd of savages rescued by God and guided to a city in progress, which now was also devastated.

All of this has a motive; as we often repeat; you must always understand that God's will is not a whim; but a justification; it's cause and effect. What was expected happened; landslides, flooding and physical death; I floated along with my loved ones but we did not succumb. The tide came in; tucked and returned in a jiffy; fast, like a sheet rocked by the fierce wind. The land masses accommodated to their new foundation. The sound of the wind and the groan of the humans were heard. It was a great lesson regarding the power of God; no matter how big or small you are; our Creator is stronger and bigger; regardless of the wisdom or intellect, strength, and technological advancement of humankind; it can be snatched in a moment. We must remain humble; I'm not saying subjected; but with free will, and aware of our place in the scope of the universal spiritual scheme. We are all souls in evolution; sacrifices and disappointments we have sometimes, and we must accept them; thanking the opportunities to learn and ascend.

I said that we were saved by Divine Grace; joining our hands and hugging tightly we remained; creating a small human raft to accommodate our little boy. We landed violently but without major injury at a great distance from our home. The unknown location was surrounded by bushes which filtered the water; retaining some terrain with wet spaces but others, dry enough to hold us. Incredibly, we fell asleep there. You are thinking that this is a novel; it is so, but there is a purpose in my story. You lived with me; you were my wife. Let's stop at this point; it is too much for you.

March 8, 2013.

Gabriel's spirit:

In the name of Almighty God; everyone can fulfill their duties and obligations in that turbulent world. There is no good reason for anxiety, desperation, crying or complaining everything is so fleeting; we hastily move towards our meeting with the infinite, with our heavenly Father who knows what is in every heart; even if they try to cover it up or deceive others.

"Come brethren, come"; says one here; there are many loving souls assembled in these spirit sessions; Praise God! Let's leave aside discords and a rush to finish; you have to take life with equanimity; a divine calmness so as to hear the celestial chords in souls and brains. There are still some notes to be given.

Urack's spirit:

The abruptness was great for us; our steps were slow and heavy, but we still had the will to go on, because once more God; an Almighty Force that we sensed, gave us life. I always wondered; why?

It was the great puzzle and after a long time of suffering, shortages and achievements; I found the answer. My evolution! Our spiritual growth was the answer! We have all started crawling, crouching, by dragging ourselves at times. Then learning and overcoming; that is the evolution of the spirit; and willingness to act; faith to believe and the determination to persist. Now I understand that it was the first chapter in this novel as you say. It was so for you too, beloved sister; but your development was a little slower for different reasons; nonetheless you also dominated the impulses of the body. We are all chained; *"linked,"* above or below; the cord is very long and solid; all embroidering the ligaments with our love; weaving a rope with our thoughts and deeds.

I finally jumped into other incarnations; you remained a slowpoke; but we once again shared marriage; they are inexplicable things; the union of those who perceive and sense old ties. I cannot tell you more for now; I simply wish you happiness; I know that you have not had it in this lifetime, but you have complied with your love ones.

March 9, 2013.

Unknown spirit:

Yes: *"The Lord is my shepherd, He leads me…and I follow His lead, His guidance, His love trail."* Stop what you're doing now.

Gilda:
Why?

Spirit:
Because I say so.

Gilda:
Who are you?

Spirit:
You don't know me.

Gilda:
OK; tell me who you are and why are you here?

Spirit:
No.

Gilda:
Please.

Spirit:
This is silly! But, someone is pushing me, poking me to speak. Telling me that I have something important to say. I don't know about that.

Gilda:
Go on.

Spirit:
My name is Emmanuel.

Gilda:
Yes, go on.

Spirit:
I arrived from Sweden, today. I don't know how I got here! Suddenly I was listening to your reading about Jesus! I love God, Jesus and the Virgin! What you're studying, learning is important for your work; I am told to tell you.

My life is very interesting; yes it is a long tale, but full of adventure, love and lessons. So sit back and hear me out. I was born in Stockholm and come from a well to do family of professionals; with comfort galore and with little love. It was cold outside and inside. Our family was run like a business, with rules and regulations. The meals were like business meetings; no warmth and little laughter, but we survived. I grew up with little expression, was introverted with pent up feelings and emotions. I had guidelines. I felt the need to reach out, looking for emotions, warm sentiments; just plain love, but I found lust instead, perversity and decay, covered up with money, luxury and artificial beauty. Deep down I knew that all that was mistaken for real love; but at that moment that was all that was to be had.

I met her on a spring day; lovely sunny afternoon it was. She strolled before me in the esplanade. I was in my thirties; unmarried still, and she was in her twenties, unmarried also. She was with a family member, walking slowly, pacing, it seemed like she was floating; her steps were soft and slow. It caught my eye. I immediately intended to approach her, and clearly my thoughts reached her, because she turned towards me. Her eyes were green gems that twinkled. It was a spiritual recognition; I was instantly hooked. She smiled, while her aunt scolded her; but she stood her ground. I asked for her name: *"Marie Encarnatte,"* she responded. Our families knew each other, I found that out later. I also knew in my soul, that we would meet again. I gave her an indication of where to find me; I then said farewell. Soon we will continue.

March 11, 2013.

Emmanuel's spirit:

Although time is short; we will continue the story. I had some power, but I used it to my liking; I was abusive, I am sorry to say it, but I've learned, and now I'm on the way to God; the straight path of piety, kindness, and love; we all learn. These are unpleasant but yet fond memories that I am telling you; they are lessons that I want to share with my brothers in pain. Nobody is perfect in that abode; we are looking for the light to get closer to perfection, which is God. I was good, but ignorant like so many others. I did not know much of piety or charity; my upbringing was not so. It was *"Self-fulfillment" "Self-indulgence."*

Why do we waste time? Enjoy time, but by helping others; loving and growing like the lovely plants and flowers. They have only one purpose; to serve, with their beauty and properties; whether medicinal or not; they give to others. Getting back to my story; I told you that I had met her. She was radiant like the sun; a happy soul she was, but also spoiled like me. We belonged to the same social circle; but had not met until now; it was fate. At last I had a purpose, something to look for, to dream about. Someone worthwhile; remember those words. We will continue, now go with God, in peace.

March 12, 2013.

Emmanuel's spirit;

Let's see, where were we? Father, thank thee. Yes, now I remember; I arrived just like that; in a blink! And here I am speaking to you; God is truly great! I must say that you are persistent; that is good. Things get done; slowly but surely.

Well, on with my story; I was surprised by my startling encounter with someone immediately dear to me; I had never felt that way before. Therefore I looked for her, waiting anxiously for the next meeting and it occurred; soon and unexpectedly; it was God sent, I thought. Surely you believe me; although I detect that you question my name and history. I am not the same person you thought; I am not he; but his descendent, yes!!!

March 13, 2013.

Gabriel's spirit:

In the name of Almighty God; there is a beautiful feeling in you, sister; the result of the sacrifice and total surrender to love, which is God. Nothing really deters your love of God and mission, bypassing anything in your way; there are no obstacles. You're sincere; you are faithful to your convictions. Now you're pacing your steps at a better increased rate; serving God through your works. You can say it's a ministry. Determination in humans is paramount; because they are capable of getting up from the floor a million times if necessary. Nothing prevents them from his or her mission. You will have good results; search for stillness within you.

There are many artists gathered here, waiting for you to start their book. *(For many years I have wanted to compile an audio book of oral history, about Puerto Rican popular music; narrated by artists, performers and composers of different genres; that I interviewed in my radio programs, in the decades of the 1980s and 1990s.)*

March 14, 2013.

Emmanuel's spirit:

This is amazing! How we are able to communicate on a daily basis like two good friends. God is truly generous and merciful, because we are not so good; needing to learn much more; but, I'm so eager to do this. Why do you always doubt? That is really a big problem; forget about the question marks: why not do the exclamation points?

This story in very, very pretty; the secret lovers were looking forward to their next encounter; seeking each other, but the timing was off, because I had to depart to another land; I was then a military man and led a contingency. There wasn't much time to tell her, so I left on a mission to Africa; this was many centuries ago. I was a strong man with a stronger personality; almost brutal and despicable in my ways. My meeting with Marie had unknowingly softened me: now, for the first time in my life, I thought about not hurting other people's feelings. This new attitude was helping me with my subjects; there was more respect and less fear.

Understand this sister; these entire stories are given to you not for entertainment, but for learning. All of us have one goal; sharing our miseries and happiness in order to guide our brothers and sisters in the right direction; so they may make better choices in their earthly incarnations. We are all still learning, it is not over yet, we can approach and share with you, due to our connection with the planet Earth. I'm looking forward to moving on, up to another level; this is an assignment; like homework.

Your good disposition is helpful and when all of this is done; you'll experience many blissful moments. Back to my story; my trip seemed endless and it finally came to an end after two bloody years. I had been hurt and limped; but still I thought about her. Arriving home my desire to see Marie was overwhelming and my search began. At that time people did not live long; many illnesses attacked the children; young mothers and the elderly were struck down with plagues. I was told that Naadia had passed away giving birth, just a few months before I arrived. She had been induced into marriage, as was the custom. We will continue.

March 15, 2013.

Gabriel's spirit:

Thinking about Almighty God makes us happy, and grateful for so many blessings in different boxes. We owe ourselves to each other; now and forever; no one progresses alone; there are always invisible allies stretching out a hand. It is a concept so simple and yet so difficult to transmit to our selfish and alienated brothers and sisters. We want to be true to our convictions; so we can sleep in peace and wake up with a desire to work; that happens to you Gilda; so control your pace so you don't waste your natural resources. The energy from others equally affects your disposition so you struggle with your sleep.

All this is happening rapidly; but for you it is slow; think about the commitment that is being fulfilled.

Emmanuel's spirit:

Dear Jesus help me; I was very devoted, and skidded; repentant I am, and I want to do well, it is my only goal; to repair injustices and ease sorrows. Let me continue Gilda. I am Emmanuel: I didn't forget that we have an obligation to end my story. We left it with the passing of my beloved Marie; I was sorrowful, devastated, as you can imagine, but I knew I'd see her again. In the battlefield her image invigorated me; even when feeling faint, her smile encouraged me. We were one, even if we weren't one in that life. What do you think? Our past as free spirits had converged many times, and we requested to be together in that existence, but could not. I felt her presence while forced to go on living. My family from society, as hers, gave me empty opulence.

I lived until an advanced age; consoled only by knowing that by dying I would find her; that's how much I loved that soul. Loving well preserves the treasures of our souls; nothing in the Universe is lost; everything is rescued by that Creator. All reverts back to us; because our Creator in his mercy knows what we need; when and if we deserve it. I lived much and suffered more; always waiting for the reunion. At last reaching the final day of that sterile life and closing my eyes I felt her warmth close by, and reopening them in spirit I saw her face and her perfume enveloped me. It was my beloved Marie who received me. We are together in infinity as we wanted; recalling our many previous encounters and our agreement to meet again. There are so many luminous details of our love, sister, that it will keep for your next book.

It is an accurate, irrefutable fact that we live, as we want to live; we look for the way, it is in our hands to make good use of our incarnations. God allows us to return and return accompanied by love ones, but always, always, it depends on how we handle our lives. Obviously Marie and I could not share that life but we now know why and it is justified. We are happy because we are together and very eager to live on a larger scale, closer to God; Amen.

March 16, 2013.

Gabriel's spirit:

In the name of Almighty God, all of us here; implore your forgiveness Father, if we have failed, if we have stumbled; we are fragile and weak and at times we believe we're strong and powerful. We ask for your blessing, Father; your mighty hand guides us, encourages and stimulates us to continue with our work; because there is much to do; and for many. There is always something to hold on to, if we believe in God. Those who doubt are poor souls that slide without support; they continue down the slide; always descending, until they recognize their mistakes and ask for forgiveness, in order to get out of the mud and at last begin their task. It is advice for those constantly wondering and asking the why of their hopelessness. Similar questions will always be there and replies too; simply by inquiring, it is a desire to amend.

Albert's spirit:

Dearest Gilda I am hugging you; along with your mom, Helena and many more; we are a loving group, you already know that. We will conclude a few stories, but soon we will close this chapter; the books such be published soon. Be calm, rest and finish your work. We love you without limits. God bless you all; I love you.

March 17, 2013.

Gabriel's spirit:

In the name of Almighty God; we do not know how many wonderful things can happen from one moment to the next, and so it is; God is always surprising us; but it really works well, when one thinks positive and with love; then the surprises are pleasant. Although sometimes, human beings cannot explain the reverses of fortune and the obstacles that also arise, but you must see it all through a positive and loving prism. Everything comes from God; and He is never wrong; we own nothing, but have everything with Him.

Unknown spirit:

To begin with, a very cordial greeting to the world, or the worlds; here and there. Sister, many souls love and respect you. From affluence to poverty; such is life on Earth; there may be a change at any time; the Poles can change in an instant; showing the power of the Creator. That is why we must be humble and grateful every day of our incarnations; savoring the joy with family, friends and with your means of support; yes, because those revenues provide your needs.

The purpose of this narration is very simple; no matter in what century you find yourself or in whichever revolving circumstances; there are constant reunions that cheer us up immensely. Centuries may pass by but we are like children, in search of our parents, siblings and friends. Sometimes we encounter villains from our past dramas; as trials or punishment for both. Whatever it may be; we must love that Creator who took pity on us; with our foolishness and pettiness that we all have. The universal stairs are very high and there are many steps; we must climb them slowly and with pauses to avoid losing our equilibrium; and then tumbling down into nothingness. We have all known each other and shared in the good and the worse; and look at us now; working together once again; each one in a different dimension. God is that great and wise!

Gilda; you were my sister; not in the life just narrated; but in one after that; my story is linked to another one given before. Think, analyze and you'll arrive at your conclusions.

March 18, 2013.

Gabriel's spirit:

In the name of Almighty God; peace and love for all those united here by love and a desire to improve this harmful world of passions and vice. Every day new apostles are needed; yes, the new messengers and laborers of love and faith. Karym *(My son)* and his young friend like him, want to help and will succeed; they are preparing to go into the world with messages of love and benevolence. It is beautiful to see the young in action with both enthusiasm and love for God and His laws. Let us pause to allow the entry of a brother also with a loving message.

Unknown spirit:

Life sometimes surprises us, and also betrays us; because we expect something; and then there is a setback coming from nowhere and getting in the way. I was looking for the light and found myself with darkness. How is that? Very easy, I went the wrong way. I had the option to follow the straight path but opted for the easy route, the dark road. It happens to many who are not evil, but reckless and stubborn; they do not listen to advice, and when the time comes they say sadly: *"Too late,"* but there is always hope and reparation; even if it takes a long time. We all have in our hands options; good or bad, to the right or to the left. You are the conductor of your soul, or the copilot; because your captain lets you make decisions.

You must open your eyes, to see the road well, avoiding the bumps, the rocks and cliffs. All that can be achieved in one lifetime or another; it's wonderful for our evolution and progress; God always gives us another opportunity. We should not waste time on pettiness and foolishness and focus only on the task today; which leads us to tomorrow; but well done, accomplished, not poorly or badly done. Finally the great redemption and a celebration will come, in the eternal world with our love ones from all eternity. Praise God!

March 19, 2013.

Gabriel's spirit:

In the name of Almighty God; I don't know why you worry so; this is not a life; it is agony. Clarity in your thoughts Gilda; serenely put the anxiety aside; remain concentrated on your work.

Life goes on whether you weep or not; it's better to live it joyfully. Stop thinking and scavenging; calm down that restless mind. Surrender to the luminousness of God. How? Let me explain something very simple and healthy for you and all. No maze is disassembled in one day; you can begin untying the threads and entanglements in a day; but to set it totally free, it is delayed in accordance with your knowledge, and spiritual and mental agility.

Once more we are talking about the lack of peace, patience and sanity; they are all tools to untangle the maze; that by the way; was forming for a long time. It did not happen from one moment to another; and was created by you; it can be fixed with God's help and the inspiration from your allies, the spirits. The wrath, discord and anger go out the window! That does not help at all; instead it's an obstacle and is detrimental to your health. Start putting your house in order. We love you.

March 20, 2013.

Unknown spirit:

I don't know what happened to me? I'm slow; willing to work, but I feel slow. Laziness is a sad thing in any world or condition; you stop doing and you sink. There is always an excuse to forget; it's the easiest way! Life becomes a nothing; thus I have lost many evolutions; great opportunities for progress because I have been idle; I'm ashamed to admit it; because now I understand my failure. God will forgive me; it's not being bad, just lazy and indifferent; until one day you realize your nothingness! You cry and have a temper tantrum about your ignorance, it is so. I am and I've been lazy but God's mercy has given me a new opportunity. I've been given a new agenda; prepared by God and sent with his messengers; I must start soon, very soon. I will go back to that density called Earth, to work; which I did not do: I wasted my time miserably. That is a very common thing. Now I have to seize the moment, not squander it. This is the commitment. I'm ready, but ask for the support of my brothers with prayers. God is kindly. Thank you for listening to me, Gilda.

March 21, 2013.

Unknown spirit;

Praise God in Heaven, and all humans of good will; I feel eternal love. Progress and charity are my goals; I am very clear about that; and you? We already know that your intentions are noble but you have to polish them; outline them well, because they're a little murky; it's like a picture that should de delineated well and with precise details. A well done sketch gives good results. You still don't understand? That is very typical of human beings; but they learn to stipulate their works over the years. Each one takes off on their own; that we also know, but when it comes to the truth; you need the support and the communion of thoughts to settle and stabilize, in other words, we need each other; that includes the two worlds. It is the encounter of two worlds; as the discovery of the new world. Every day we discover something new; ours is an eternal search, but it has results if we persist in the inquiry. No excuses or laments; our work must be tangible, so when we give our accounts to the Creator, we can show a task well done.

March 22, 2013.

Gabriel's spirit:

In the name of Almighty God; no one is exempt from suffering in this world. There are minor and major ties with other humans that impose duties and obligations which are often very painful and uncomfortable. All of that is part of the commitments; we must abide by it. With you Gilda, it is a very different case; your picked your tests; knowing the many debts that you've entered into, in your multiple incarnations. God has rewarded you for your discipline and devotion in this life; since very young. So little remains to do; don't fail.

Another unknown spirit:

Gilda Mirós, I am very present; with all my irons. I am a musician and I live in spirit musically, with the joy of having brought happiness and rhythm to the world. I encourage you dear sister; go get it!!!

March 23, 2013.

(I had received the following message on September 5, 2007. It was misplaced and I didn't find it until now.)

Fabio's spirit:

The data that I'm going to give is true, it's not fiction; be patient with yourself, and with the task. Peace and love, sister. Brazil, it was Brazil; where there are great believers and laborious people. Praise God! My name is Fabio; I was a peasant, working on my family's farm since my parent's death. I became an orphan as a child, but had a large and loving extended family; they were good to me, I cannot complain about my childhood, because I lacked nothing.

I lost my mother's care first and then ten years after my father's. I had no brothers, but many cousins. We were true believers in spiritism; some were mediums. It was our custom to meet once a week to pray. We had a good relationship with the spirits, as well as you.

Fabio's spirit: *(Fabio reappeared now, after six years.)*

We are many here; the room is full, as your brother Nel always says; God protect him; bless him for his great love, peace and nobility. My history is incomplete; I am Fabio; believe it; that is always your impediment. I had told you about my upbringing in a large family in Brazil, with much love and comfort even though we were not wealthy, but great believers, and there were a couple of mediums. My country vibrates in spirit and music. We are happy despite great poverty; social inequality is enormous; although there seems to be an improvement; they are more aware of the spirit. It's about the love of life and how to improve the daily living. I would sing while I worked and I worked a lot; first in the farm and then in the city. As a child, I learned that the hours fly if you sing; it is easier if you keep happy even with the obstacles which arise constantly in shapes of people and events; there is always something to complain about.

Later, as a grown up in the city of hustle and bustle Rio, I followed my artistic impulses as a painter, yes, a painter. I painted the sky, the fields; I painted my cheerful child experiences even though being an orphan. Festive were my paintings; I draw well and injected my love with color to all my work. I had success; imagine! I sold my works to tourists. What a delight when I saw that they were carrying a bit of me in my paintings;

It's an extraordinary sensation, selling my painting; not for the money; for the recognition. My spirit wanted to jump out of my skinny body. I was not attractive, rather charismatic and likeable; like most of my countrymen; the smile is always on their lips. Stay calm, sister.

March 24, 2013.

Gabriel's spirit:

In the name of Almighty God; let's not underestimate the power of love and prayer; it is a very powerful combination. The environment around you changes when you pray; beneficial fluids come from infinity, spirit relatives can approach and the Divine Grace envelopes you. Everything is possible with love and prayer.

Fabio's spirit:

That was a pretty introduction; and so true. I am Fabio; we have a commitment and up to now, have not failed. As I was saying; I was a painter, but also restless; I was passionate about life. No, I didn't do anything wrong; on the contrary, I sought to do good deeds; I helped the poor with my meager income. I learned something very important; it's not how much, or how you do charity to your brothers; but it's about attitude. There should be no humiliation, nor expecting compensation or rewards; do it simply for the joy of sharing. Something beautiful and surprising happened to me; one day I saw an old man crossing a noisy and active street in my beautiful city; but the man was in danger because his old age made him slow and a bit disoriented. I ran to help and just saved him from a terrible accident.

The elderly man looked at me with gratitude. I assisted him and we started talking; he told me of his loneliness and I told him of mine; I understand now that it was a predestined meeting. Escorting him to his little room; we had coffee. I went there often to visit him; he became family. Soon I drew him, because his facial features were intriguing and very interesting to me. I didn't do "*Portraits,*" but him I did; surprising me how well that painting turned out.

Another day, heading home I met a beautiful woman; that was also charitable; she visited homeless families. We started talking and my interest in her went much beyond the usual. I will tell you that I loved life. These two events are linked, believe it or not; because humans, seek and find each other, when least expected; God guiding, sending us on.

The old man suddenly died from a heart attack but there was his painting; he looked alive; that's how well I had painted him; I spoke to him and prayed for him. His spirit manifested itself one good day; I saw and heard him. You know that I was a believer, I was a spiritist. The spirit said to me: *"My son, I was your father in the past and in this life I had no children but your complied with me; fulfilling a promise you had made to me then; to take care of me; you did it. Promises and debts are eternal; they are impregnated in infinity, and sooner or later they are made good; I am at peace and grateful. I love you, good son."* His words stayed within my soul and I thanked God that I could fulfill my promise.

March 25, 2013.

Gabriel's spirit: *(I was reading the Gospel.)*

Illumination and progress Gilda; what you are reading is beautiful and educational; much good is does to your soul a bit in conflict by the vicissitudes of life, especially your daily routine. Harmony in everything is paramount; that applies to work and to leisure. We all have sacred commitments as you have noticed by our many messages; its good knowing the commitments are completed. Our souls will dance and sing in a spiritual euphoria with the love of God, when we get there; achieving our goals. So it will also be for you, sister.

Fabio's spirit:

Let me continue my story; it is very beautiful, it has surprises and good lessons. I feel very satisfied to be able to tell it to the world, for the readers to know of the Divine Mercy that is God. It has been said many times that nothing is lost in the Universe; especially love, that is eternal. Suddenly you meet up with a great lost love, or a deed of sincere love, a charitable act or a hand you gave to a friend, and a word of consolation in time. All that remains; nothing is lost and we can rescue it, if it goes astray. What does that mean? That the intentions must be good, honorable and if it was not, it can be rectified. You can apologize for an improper intention. God gave us free will and that saves us; rectifying and correcting our negativity attitudes into positive; the indifference into affection. My whole story consists of that. The beautiful woman I eventually sought; conquering my heart even with a disability, made me very happy; becoming the mother of my two children and fulfilling all duties as a wife.

That soul had also known me in a previous life; she was very beautiful and good, but I had been a tyrant to her; and even then she loved and forgave me. Now it was my part to be docile, comprehensive, patient and tolerant. I had a debt with her, and our love that survived time. My wife understood and accepted my spiritist belief; she sensed our past and thanked God, as I did, for giving us a new opportunity to unite our souls once more. We reached old age together; she was blind by then and I cared for her, and with great love I did it. We are now together and happy with our revelation to you; and eager to write the next chapter in a new incarnation. Thank you Father.

March 26, 2013.

Gabriel's spirit:

In the name of Almighty God; believe me dearest Gilda; it's not worth living without faith in God, Many say that they don't believe, but their souls cry out for help; looking to cling on to something so as not to sink into the swamp of filth. They don't believe because they have not opened the door to God love; He's there knocking; waiting for them to let him in.

Many know the beauty of love; because we feel it, by practicing it; love is an integral part of the spiritual being, but like a muscle, it has to be exercised, otherwise it weakens. Each time it gets easier when you work with love; It gives us the clarity and ability to think and execute; it's so, so simple. Gilda, what you are all living, is love reciprocated; every day there are more and more responses to love and faith that all of you have. We can say that it is a loving chain that binds, leading you to a sort of happiness; that is never complete there, but that it makes this evolution more tolerable. This new cycle of more peace and rewards just started, and as your son Karym says; *"And there is still more to come, dear Gilda."*

March 27, 2013.

Gabriel's spirit:

In the name of Almighty God; what more can we ask God for? We have so much; we are rich, having each other; our love is worth much, much more than money in the bank. Dearest Gilda; your mind is a jumping bean; you have to quiet down. There are good days and disturbing ones; but we must maintain our spiritual composure in harmony every single day; with storms, lightning, rain or shine; everything depending on the harmony maintained by you. No one can guarantee us peace; you have to look for it, get it and protect it, like a baby in your arms; for that peace will grow as the child and will give you the riches of the soul which are eternal.

We make our lives restless; with anxieties and imbalance and we forget what is essential in our lives. We spirits bring messages as prompters: *"Reminders,"* so that you may dress up in love, peace, faith and hope; which are the best clothes; the ideal wardrobe; suitable for all occasions. Leave aside the nonsense; these harmful habits that belittle. Although the river may sound; you as a good fisherman stay in a nook, waiting for the storm to pass; knowing that everything passes. We have a few more pages to do, and I'll give you my farewell to this work. My brothers and sisters are always willing; and also thank you for your disposition.

March 28, 2013.

Gabriel's spirit:

In the name of Almighty God; we are all here; together as always, helping you; loving you, and watching so that the boys fulfill their obligations; they are good and always think of us; they know that we aid them and they are grateful. Thank you Almighty Father for allowing these communications, which are blessed by Thee. There are few meetings like these; there are variants, but we know that ours is very special and that pleases us and makes us extremely happy.

Unknown spirit:

Dear friend; who I am, it doesn't matter in the least; my message is important. I bring my baskets; as Helena says, full of goodies for everyone, here and there. I am as Saint Nick; I like to give presents. We know that everyone asks for something; there is always a need and we the angel messengers bring answers and gifts for humankind. We only ask for peace in souls, in the hearts and clarity in the brains. You can say it's a divine loving exchange. Yes, calm down, quietly, so you may well receive my message; progress we want for everyone; it is the goal. Life pushes us from one side to another, but we must have strength to sustain the bumps and shocks. Not brute force; I speak of faith, which keeps us in place.

"Streaming" is what the medium's perispirit is receiving from the spirit; it is a live signal. That's a new term now, but it is older than the wind; because the spirits communicate projecting their thoughts, their frequency, to the human being with the readiness to receive it; which is the receptor.

Now science finally confirms the many choices in communications; in either world. Everything, is based on frequency and energy; invisible to the human eye; but with many susceptible humans that capture it.

(From Wikipedia; the free encyclopedia.)
Streaming media *is multimedia that is constantly received by and presented to an end user while being delivered by a provider. Its verb form, "to stream", refers to the process of delivering media in this manner; the term refers to the delivery method of the medium rather than the medium itself.*

It is necessary to disclose all this in a simple way; and that's where human beings like you come in, Gilda; thank you for your good will. Changes will arrive; great and good. Continue little sister with your enthusiasm; writings you have, and you will have more.

Helena's spirit:

Dearest sister, it's Helena; yes little sister; do not doubt it Gilda, do not hesitate. This is a very special messenger; we are honored with his presence today, and we are all grateful. He leaves a clear and strong aura of pure energy from another region. Thank him and thank God. Finalizing this work, there will be a wide and very pretty road; we will enter it together like a caravan of goodness. Peace and love to all.

March 29, 2013.

Gabriel's spirit:

In the name of Almighty God; Gilda, don't judge anyone by your principles, let them judge themselves; everyone has a conscience; everyone understands the rules of good conduct; I speak of the spirit. It is our conscience that speaks to us every minute; it's a lie detector; we have spiritual fire alarms that warn us of unhealthy passions; selfishness and envy. All those tools are in us; we are born with our safety equipment, giving us protection; but over the years we stopped listening to them and they spoiled; it stops working and then there is a tragedy. We burn ourselves in our own flames; although the alarm sounds to let us know. The worst blind person is he or she that doesn't want to see or hear; that is certainly true with the hardened spirit.

Good sister; this book is almost finished and we, once again, thank each of the benevolent, self-sacrificing and hardworking brothers and sisters who have worked with us; it's as you say; a *"Joint Endeavor;"* a work by a group; it will remain for centuries and centuries. Your brother is quite right; you will have many more messages; for your next work; there are numerous spirits, musical souls, waiting to make their entrance with their instruments. All of this occurs with God's permission.

April 1, 2013.

Gabriel's spirit:

In the name of Almighty God; dearest Gilda, how well you understand us, with simply a few words. That is the affinity that you had with your Mom, and look how far we have come with this understanding and telepathy between spirits. We are confident that it will be full of productive tips and sincere love for the suffering world: with God everything is possible.

Why are we always asking for illumination? Because in the darkness we stumble and it becomes difficult to find the door or the way; to be in the dark is a sad thing; there are so many cracks and altercations. We must strengthen the spirit as we do the body; when we take vitamins and tonics as invigorators or exercise; health for both, body and soul is important; essential for the progress of the spirit in evolution. The best vitamin is prayer; and the exercise is to do charitable acts with words, deeds and thoughts. There is nothing to fear; the fog is dissipating; there are always new goals.

April 3, 2013.

Gabriel's spirit;

In the name of Almighty God; asking for enlightenment and progress for you dear Gilda. Everything is ready over here; the banquet is almost served waiting for the grand celebration and the many guests. There are multicolored streamers and tassels that Helena brought, dances and music coordinated by Monserrate and skits and recitations that Albert organized. All that and much more; flowers, fragrances, lights, and above all joy in the souls who have completed a task. Let's not forget the incense and the candles that Gilda likes.

Helena's spirit:

Peace and love dearest sister; you started the day serenely and here we are with you; all is well; you'll see the good results in several ways. Yes, Yes, it's me, Helena; visiting you again with great joy. Both books are ready; can you believe it? That's wonderful! Thank you Father; and thank the brothers who have assisted you. *"Lina" (Nickname)* you finally learned.

Yes, there is much more in different ways. Who knew? It is a great feat for all. Your mother Monserrate is doing a Can Can; it's a celebration!

There are many beautiful things in life, if we look for them and enjoy them; it is a question of appreciation. Every moment can be beautiful; when viewed with a divine light. With God's lighthouse darkness becomes illumination and harmony. It is flipping the face of the coin; it's reversing the negative to positive with our thoughts, attitudes and goodwill. We all have that power; it's free and it's in us; it is an internal lantern. The generator is the love of God and the engine is your faith; working in unison. You can see how easy it is to understand that happiness is within us; our happiness is in our hands. Hold on to it; do not lose it! Grab it, cherish it, protect it and share it.

April 5, 2013.

Gabriel's spirit:

In the name of Almighty God; sister, imagine a garden with beautiful flowers, scents and fragrances unknown on Earth. A cool breeze caresses your face and brings more scents from a distance. A bright sun is shining and there are also several moons and planets in sight. Birds chirp their melodious and harmonious songs; fruits abound in different colors, sizes and flavors. Multicolored fish and animals jump with joy in their natural environments. Everyone feels God's presence in the air, the trees, in the mountains and rivers. He is the spiritual oxygen we inhale; it is He who makes us vibrate; dream and progress. There is no dissension or discord; all is harmonious; it is intimate happiness, very typical of each and all.

There's understanding and compassion, and a burning desire of benevolence; we want to gain knowledge and reach the summit together. Nobody is lazy or lustful; we are all industrious and clean of soul and body. What I describe dear sister is only a part of the beauty that exists in our world of the spirit. It is difficult to describe it well with human words, because the atmosphere, the feelings, the emotions and the joys are indescribable.

This postscript is to encourage our brothers on Earth, as they wait to discarnate; which is the change from the physical to the spirit body; with peace and joy. Calmness helps the demise of the body and aids the accommodating entities waiting for them. As much as I say, it's not enough, but it leaves a question mark and curiosity in everyone that reads this page; that was our mission.

Gilda, the end does not exist in any world; it's always rewinding; it's undertaking a voyage once more. We are all ready to continue with our sacred missions and long-lasting commitments. The disposition and the spiritual forces necessary to complete the goals are there. We stride along surveying; tossing aside debris and collecting the treasures of the soul. Thank you Father; we love you.